TOUCHED

by
my

Father

A HEALING
JOURNEY

TIMOTHY
JAMES
AVERY

TOUCHED BY MY FATHER:

A HEALING JOURNEY

ISBN (978-1-0968-9088-1)

Printed in the USA by
Kindle Direct Publishing

<u>Dedication:</u>

This book is dedicated to my mom and sisters who are the epitome of overcomers.

Acknowledgements:

First, I want to thank my Lord and Savior Jesus Christ, to whom all the glory of this book is given. He has put this book on my heart to write. He has been and will always be in every moment of my life working through horrible tragedies and turning them into good. None of this book would be possible without His love, grace, mercy, and redemptive power. If He is not a part of your life, I hope, that by the end of my book, you will make him your Lord and Savior, too.

I want to thank my beautiful and loving wife, Dawna Starr Avery. She has graciously and patiently helped me to craft this hard story to tell. Dawna has loved me through the pain that I caused her. She is an incredible wife and a true gift from God. She has been a rock of encouragement and a compass to help keep my focus on God. Dawna is a true helpmate in every sense of the word.

I want to thank my daughter Sophia. She has loved me unconditionally and has allowed me to be a father to her. She has encouraged her mother and me to be the best that God has called us to be.

I want to thank my mother-in-love, Dianna Rutland, who has been one of my biggest cheerleaders. She has been incredibly supportive in me in many ways. I am deeply grateful for her.

I want to give a special thanks to our friends, Janie Levine and Sherrie Benoit Chatelain (Benoit Design and Photography), who have been so gracious in assisting with my book. Thank you, Katie Lancaster, @ktfotography for the photography skills.

To the fathers in my life who God used to mold me.

- Lewis Rutland, my father-in-love, was used in healing many father wounds by showing me how a father should love a son.

- Pastor Joey Turner, thank you for being on the phone with my father and me ready to give him an opportunity to receive the Lord.

- Dr. Randal Langley, my spiritual father and mentor, has encouraged me to be the man that God has called me to be and provided sound counsel and wisdom through the years.

- Don Valley, the counselor and accountability partner God used to help me break free from believing the lies of the enemy. You have been a compassionate and patient friend.

- Scott McGihon, a steadfast leader, mentor, and a great friend. Your passionate example for men to love their families has been inspiring to witness.

"Powerful stories of God's faithfulness in the difficult moments of life. Even greater are the stories of triumph over trials that took years. Tim found God's faithfulness and His imprints when looking back on those seasons when Tim felt all alone or abandoned. Timeless truths for anyone's darkest hours and a powerful testament to the faithfulness of God. Tim and his wife, Dawna, don't just teach it---they have walked through every step of the way and have lived to tell the stories and extend hope and light to those drowning in dark places."

Dr. Rich Rogers
Editorial Director of **Kingdom Connection**
Jentezen Franklin Ministries
www.jentezenfranklin.org

Foreword

Brave. Powerful. Raw. Real. Authentic. Heart-Wrenching. Humble. These are all words that came to mind as I read "Touched By My Father" by Tim Avery. I have to be honest, my "father's heart" was broken and I was challenged to the max as I found myself weeping several times as I read this book. Most men in today's culture would try to hide their humiliation, brokenness, and wounds. But not Tim Avery! Tim's genuine passion to see people healed and restored is the driving force behind this book. You can "hear" Tim's heart with clarity as he tells his personal story... a story that ends with a beautiful picture of redemption and restoration back to a relationship with our Heavenly Father. Sadly, this is a story that many will directly relate to. My prayer is that those who read this book will find great courage and determination to begin their own personal pursuit of healing and wholeness. It's been a great joy to walk with Tim over the past few years. I've watched him pursue his God-given calling and grow as a man, husband, and father. I couldn't be more proud of a spiritual son than I am with Tim and this work. No, it's not polished and professional (in the sense of a big budget book production). But it IS POWERFUL, TRUE and LIFE GIVING! Please join me in helping to get this book into the hands of those who are in desperate need of God's love and grace.

Dr. Randal S. Langley, President
Christian Life School of Theology Global
www.clstglobal.org
www.clstgo.com

TABLE OF CONTENTS:

PREFACE

Father, Jesus, and Holy Spirit help me to tell our story in a way that those who read it not only see your loving pursuit for me but for them as well. I want them to see that although I resisted You, You were there still pursuing and protecting me. I want this book to point to You, Jesus. You have shown me the truth of where You were in every one of my situations which allowed freedom to flow and Your truth to overtake the lies of the enemy. True freedom only exists in Your Kingdom and can exist in our lives when we dethrone ourselves and submit to You as our King. Help us to see the error in our ways of thinking that freedom is when we make our own decisions based on our own understanding rather than trusting Your guidelines for living a freedom-filled life. This can only come when we fully accept Your free gift of salvation and fully surrender to Your process of sanctification. Thank You, Jesus.

Chapter 1
Eden

We all know the story of Adam and Eve. The beautiful and perfect paradise in which they lived. They got to experience an intimate relationship with God that we cannot fully comprehend on this side of heaven. God walked with Adam in the cool of the day. Adam knew what God looked like. God gave Adam the whole world to rule and to have dominion over. Adam had a partnership with God in naming all the animals. It says in the Bible that ALL the beasts of the land, air, and sea submitted to Adam and Eve. He gave Adam and Eve and the animals plenty of food to eat. They all shared from the same food source. Every living creature was a vegetarian. Adam and Eve had no enemies. They ruled the world. Think about this for a moment; to know of a world that is so peaceful that war never existed. Death or disease is not a concern because you never heard of it. Think about not having to worry if someone was lying to you or if they had a hidden agenda to get you to do something. Think about the simple fact that lying doesn't exist. A world where everything you hear is true, and there is no reason to question it because there is no need to doubt it. Everything just was or is. You live in a perfect world. Trust has no contrast to compare it to. Everything you see, smell, touch, taste, and hear is good. The absolute good. Not a good, better, or best. Just the absolute meaning of good.

Adam and Eve didn't know what wrong, mistrust, hurt, pain, or what sorrow was. Remember they didn't even know they were naked; they had no shame. They had no concept of "wrong" or "evil." Adam and Eve only knew what was given to them and presented to them to live. In other words, they had no choice but to live in a place prepared for them. Why? Because they had not eaten from the tree of the knowledge of good and evil... yet. Think about this. they couldn't fully comprehend "good" without the contrast of "evil".

This, I believe, is the sense of innocence and purity in which we are all born into this world. In our childlike innocence, we trust everything and everybody. In our naivety, we think that it's okay to talk to anyone and everyone. That is, until our parents tell us not to talk to strangers, to look both ways before crossing the street and, to hold their hand while in the store. Not fully understanding our parents' rules, we reluctantly obeyed. We trust our parents because we know they love and want to protect us. In that same innocent mindset, let's say that a child discovers something about their body that was meant to be enjoyed later in life.

2

How, as a parent of that child, would you handle explaining your child's discovery? I experienced sexual arousal at a very young age. Though I did not fully understand the sensation - I enjoyed it because it felt good. I'll get to my story in just a moment. But first, I want to ask a follow-up question. If your child was aroused, would you explain to them that this sensation was a good thing or a bad thing? God made our body, and He said that it was "good," shouldn't everything that our body experiences be good? What happens when someone knows that tickling you made you laugh? They would tickle you, right?!

When my nephew was younger, he loved to be tickled. He would squirm and giggle in anticipation! Even when I raised my hands and wiggled my fingers in his sight, he would start to giggle. He associated the movement of my fingers to being tickled.

So, even at the thought of being tickled, he would start to squirm and giggle. He knew that the sensation of being tickled produced laughter and laughter made him feel good. He knew his uncle was a source of that sensation. When he saw me, he knew he was going to be tickled. My nephew is older now, and even to this day when he sees me, he still smiles and can't help but to laugh.

Now, what about pain? Can we associate people with pain? Sure! We know being pinched or slapped makes

3

us wince in pain. What if a person we know slaps us or pinches us in every encounter that we see them and that person knew that by doing so, it made us feel fear towards them. We would associate that person with pain and fear, right?! We would want nothing to do with that person. We would conclude that this person was bad and evil. Even the sight of that person would strike fear and pain in our bodies. Therefore, by understanding this information, if a person wanted to be associated with the sensation of fear or joy in one's life, they would know how to do that, right?!

What if someone you trusted knew how to stimulate you sexually and they wanted you to see them as the source of that sensation? You would go back to that person to feel that sensation again, especially if it was your first experience. Given this information, would you say that being sexually stimulated was a good or bad thing? More than likely you would want more information. You would want to ask more questions to get clarity of the circumstances. We all know that in the context of marriage the answer to that question is a resounding, "Good thing." What if you were a child in this situation? What if that person were the same gender as you? What if that person were your parent? The answer changes according to the circumstance that surrounds the experience. So, even though the experience may be a horrible one, is the 'sensation' of being sexually stimulated a bad thing? I think the 'sensation' of sexual stimulation is a good thing.

Let me explain and rest assured I'm not condoning sexual immorality, incest, rape, molestation, prostitution, homosexuality, or pornography. What I am saying is that God, our Creator created the 'sensation' of sexual arousal as good. God created all five sensations: seeing, hearing, tasting, smelling and touching. Sex is good; it falls into the category of touch. God gave it to us to enjoy. However, it has to be used in the way it was designed to experience the full potential of its pleasure. I believe the first experience of sexual stimulation imprints in our minds of what sex is, regardless if the experience is good or bad.

That's why I want to lay the foundation that the 'sensation' of sexual stimulation is good; it is a gift from God. Therefore, your response to such stimulation is also good. What we need to do is investigate and understand the 'circumstances' and 'intentions' leading up to the sexual arousal. Were they good or bad?

Today, most people's first sexual encounter will not be experienced on their wedding night. More often than not, people who struggle with their sexual identity or have sexual addictions have had their first experience of sexual stimulation as a young child. They were never taught the reasons for their newfound sensation and what it is used for. Or worse yet, this sensation was discovered because a trusted person touched them inappropriately.

We have no choice in the matter of the hand that we are dealt. The life that we are born into was not of our choosing. Neither do I think that our life is of a random occurrence. I believe every life was ordered with a purpose. God has given us free will to follow him or not.

Now, on to my story. For the privacy and protection of some of the people in my life, I have changed certain names. Parents and adults, let me preface this with saying that the next few chapters of my story may be difficult to read. I encourage you to read it first before sharing it with your sons and daughters.

Chapter 2
Molestation

My dad was a supply sergeant in the U.S. Army and stationed at Andrews Air Force Base in Maryland. We lived in Forestville, Maryland. My mother, born and raised in Germany, met my father while he was stationed in Germany. I was the middle child and the only boy sandwiched between two girls. At the ages of seven, six and three, we all got along pretty well as siblings.

My Opa (grandfather), Heinz, flew in from Germany in the summer of 1988 to spend some time getting to know his grandkids. My mom worked late hours making pizzas at a local pizza place. My father would usually get home after five pm. So, we spent most of the day with Opa during the time of his visit. I loved my Opa. He was funny and so entertaining. I remember this one trick he did with his fingers which fooled me into believing that he had separated his thumb from one hand and slid it along the forefinger of his other hand. I lit up in disbelief. Opa then slid his supposedly severed thumb back into position and opened both hands showing that his thumb was reattached.

He'd chuckle, and I'd say, "Do it again, Opa!" He would perform the trick over and over again until he showed me how to do it myself.

"It's getting close to your bedtime son," my dad announced as he walked through the door, "and you need to take your bath." He continued into the bathroom. My father told me to get undressed while he drew the bath water. To my shock he got

Undressed, too, and flipped the shower diverter to start the shower. He helped me into the shower. Standing there he lathered himself and began lathering me. After washing off my body, he began to touch me and began fondling me. The careful (or so I thought) caressing of my six-year-old body aroused a sensation in me that I never felt before. I gasped, and he quickly moved his hands away from me. Not wanting my father to stop, I said, "*Daddy, do it again!*" My father peeked out of the bathroom door looking for the whereabouts of my Opa. Assuming the coast was clear; he put his finger over his mouth and said, "*Shhh!*" I knew then in my young mind I was to keep this a secret.

After that day, I recall myself wanting to feel that new sensation of pleasure again, but how I wondered? One day as I was lying on my stomach playing with my toys, I felt a stimulation as I pressed myself on the floor that emulated the sensation I experienced in the shower with my father. Not fully understanding what I was doing, I continued to do it because it felt good. The door of sexual perversion had been opened.

Before this encounter, I can't recall a time when my father hurt me. I loved being around him. He'd tuck me in at night and sing me to sleep. I knew he loved me; he had my complete trust. I had no reason to think that what my Dad did to me in the shower was wrong or evil. For all I knew, he was teaching me something new.

My father did; he awoke a sensation in me that I didn't know existed and I wanted more of it.

Let's go back to our story in Eden. The serpent knew God told Adam and Eve they would die upon eating the fruit. Therefore, the serpent had to appeal to the benefits of the forbidden fruit, and make it seem that God was holding this back from them. The serpent said, "*You won't die. In fact, God knows that when you eat of it your eyes will be opened and you'll be like God knowing Good and Evil.*" the serpent said. So, because it was going to make them like God, they took and ate of the fruit.

However, as soon as they bit into the fruit, a flood of new information coursed through their brains. Overwhelmed by the overload of new information they felt shame. They knew they were naked. The Bible recounts they sewed fig leaves together to hide their nakedness. They were ashamed of being naked. Let's pause and expound on this. Who told Adam and Eve that being naked was wrong? Was it God? No. He created their bodies and said that it was good. God didn't say let's create man in Our image and issue them each a robe because being naked is evil. So, did the serpent tell them that it was wrong to be naked? Nope! The Bible doesn't say the serpent told them that either. So where did they get this new revelation? They just ate the fruit that gave them the knowledge of Good and Evil. Here's what I believe happened. They were used to seeing God in the cool of the day. More likely than not, God was clothed. If they were to be like Him, good and perfect, then they needed to be clothed also. So, they concluded that nakedness needed to be covered. There it is! They concluded! They determined their Good and Evil. This brought on shame. Did you catch what God said to Adam and Eve when He questioned them? Read it Gen 3:11. He didn't ask, "Who said being naked was wrong?" He asked, "Who told you that you were naked?" Then God asks a follow-up question. "Did you eat from the tree of the knowledge of Good and Evil?" Indicating they must have come to their conclusion that nakedness was wrong. The truth in this situation is that our nakedness is good. God created us and said that it is Good. Being naked allows us to trust God by allowing Him to see every part of us. He desires intimacy or in-to-me-I-see with His creation. He wants to know and see every detail of our being. Obviously, I'm not suggesting we run around naked so God can be more intimate with us. What I'm saying is that we need to stop trying to cover up or hide from God. He wants us to be naked (transparent) before Him. It exposes our shame and guilt, so He can speak truth to our hurts and pains and set us free. More often than not, we stay hidden from Him because we think we are damaged goods, and God is ashamed of us. By remaining hidden, we justify our actions that were rooted in the tragic events of our lives which formed a prejudice and ethos of how we handle people and situations. It took me 25 years to realize this. I finally took the time to expose myself to God and allow Him to heal my father's wounds. I went to a friend who is a Christian counselor and specializes in freedom and deliverance ministry. His ministry is aptly called Restoring the Foundations. I want to share this experience with you now, and afterward, I will take you through my life journey of hiding from God.

Why share this healing part now? Because, I want you to see there is hope for you immediately if you choose. This is the freedom ministry encounter that brought healing to my first hurt.

I walked into my counselor's home office, a little nervous, not knowing what to expect. Was I going to spew pea soup? Was I going to foam at the mouth? After talking with my counselor, he reassured me nothing like that would happen. We go through praying off soul ties and renouncing any family ties to occult practices and so on. Then I asked for forgiveness of the sins that I committed, I forgave myself for doing them, and I forgave those who had hurt me. After that, I closed my eyes.

My counselor began to lead me in a series of prayers and then said, "Okay, Tim, remain there with your eyes closed and allow the Holy Spirit to take you to your first hurt."

I did so. The next thing I saw was the shower scene in my head. I'm a kindergartener showering with my dad. I can hear myself saying, "Do it again!"

The counselor asked, "What's going on? What do you see?"

"My dad touched me, and it felt good. I don't know why I'm being shown this!" I responded.

"Do you want to ask the Holy Spirit why you're being shown this?" the counselor asked.

"Holy Spirit, why am I being shown this?" I inquired.

Holy Spirit replied to me, "Your father told you that he thought you liked being touched there. As you should have, I created your body with the sensation of touch and arousal. However, this sensation is to be enjoyed in the atmosphere of marriage. Those sensations were awakened early and improperly in you. The enemy took what I created for intimacy in the marriage bed and perverted it. The seed of perversion was rooted in you at such a young age. You struggled with guilt because you enjoyed the sensation. Shame set in because you didn't know how to tell what happened without feeling guilty from the pleasure you felt. The enemy wanted this rooted in you at an early age so you would be convinced that you were born attracted to men. This has been the enemy's tactic on advancing same-sex attraction. If the enemy can be the first to awaken the sexual pleasure areas in your body, then he knows that he has a chance of perverting them and convincing people they are attracted to the same sex. Especially if the encounter happens at an age they can barely remember."

"What do you see now?" The counselor asked.

"Jesus. He is in the shower with me, and He is washing me. I can see dirt running down the drain. Jesus said that He is washing off the perverted pleasures. He is washing me clean of all my shame, guilt, and condemnation. I can see it all washing down the drain. 'Now your memory is forever changed!' declared Jesus. I then see Jesus

wrap a large towel around me. He picks me up, wrapping me in His arms, and starts to sing to me. He kisses me on my forehead and says, 'I love you, my child.' Tears began to roll down my face. I opened my eyes and knew that I was forever changed.

This one profound encounter undid decades of false beliefs that I tried to drown out with alcohol. It took me 25 years to get to this point and gain this freedom. If you had something happen to you, please for your own sake, get healing from it; even if you believe you are fine now and forgave your perpetrator. I forgave my dad too, but something was keeping me from being totally free. I still carried the guilt that 'I liked it' and that it was my fault. It was the truth revealed to me, that set me free of the shame and guilt. This is validated in John 8:32. That's what I want for you; to expose yourself to God the Father and allow Him to speak truth into your encounter so you can be set free.

What I don't want for you is what Adam and Eve did when God asked them, *"Have you eaten from the tree of which I commanded you not to eat from?"* Gen 3:11. They started to play the blame game. Adam blamed Eve. *"God, this woman that you gave me fed me the fruit."* Eve blamed the serpent. *"Lord, the serpent tricked me, and then I ate the fruit!"*

God, in turn, reprimanded all of them. We do this in most of our situations, don't we? We play the blame game. He did it, or she did it. If this hadn't happen to me, then I would be better off. In some cases, things happen to us and we have no way of controlling the situation. You could have been raped or molested like I was. You could have been abducted as a child.

You could have lost someone to the hands of a drunk driver. Things are going to happen to us. There isn't a promise of a pain-free life. We do, however, get to choose how we respond to every event that happens to us.

To describe it like "Jones," a character from the Andy Andrews' book, "*The Noticer.*" *"People are going to push you in the pool, how you respond is entirely up to you!"* Friends, although we can't control the unthinkable events in our lives, we can decide how the tragedies of our lives dictate our future. We can choose one or the other: We can choose to think we are damaged goods and blame God for not protecting us from a horrible event. Or we can choose to forgive, seek out healing and bring closure to that part of our lives so that we can move on and thrive.

Friends, we are not the sum total of the tragic events in our lives. Our lives are meant to last a lifetime, not our tragedies. Tweet that! Remember that!

This is what I want for you to learn from my story. I am a firm believer that we need to learn from each other's mistakes so that we all don't fall into the same trap. Learn how to break free from being a victim who was pushed in the pool. If you don't, you will be in a torturous cycle of reliving the offenses over and over again. Every decision you make will be through the lens of those traumatic events.

Now you are about to put on my lens of life and see through the root cause of the decisions I made. Not to justify my decisions, but to show you the consequences of not seeking healing from God.

Chapter 3
The Effect on my Childhood

The stories that I will share with you remind me of the sadness, hurt, pain, tears, disgust, anger, and most of all shame that I went through. I share them with you to bring hope and freedom to the pain that you are feeling. If you were forced, coerced or manipulated into doing something you didn't want to do or didn't know what you were doing and you are seeking healing, then keep reading. I hope these stories create a bond of unity between you and me. Especially if you have experienced something similar you know that you aren't the only one and that you too can be set free from the shame and guilt that come along with them.

After the shower encounter with my dad at age 6, the molestation continued to happen throughout my childhood years. As a result, I would repeat the behavior of masturbation throughout my childhood and into my teenage years. My mom and dad never explained to me that what I was doing was wrong nor did they tell me that the sensation that I was feeling was meant for something else. My mom was probably shocked at the behavior and didn't know what to do. My father, in his twisted mind, knew what happened and plotted another perverted encounter. Out of curiosity, and from what was awakened, I did things with my sisters that no brother and sister should ever do, incest. This behavior happened over three encounters and stopped because I knew it was wrong. If you are a parent, you need to ask questions of your son or daughter if you catch them in this behavior. Yes, it will be embarrassing on both parts, but trust me, if your child were touched inappropriately, you would want to know about that immediately! Help your kids understand their bodies. Let them know if someone touches them that it's not okay and that they need to tell mommy or daddy. It may be an awkward conversation to have, but you'll be glad you did. Can you imagine having your son or daughter tell you later at the age of 20 that they were abused and they thought that you knew and did nothing to protect them? That's what I did. I'll tell you about that later.

Pornographic Magazines

When I was seven years old, I'd walk home from school with a group of older kids. One of the kids on this particular day had taken a *Playboy* magazine from their home to show everyone. The older boys were looking at it and said to me: "*Hey, Timmy! Come look at this.*" They told me, "*If you rub yourself on it, it feels as if you are having sex with them.*" So, I took it and tried it and said, "*Yeah, I can feel it!*" Not truly understanding what sex meant in my seven-year-old mind, I just connected it to the sensation that I discovered. After that, my lust for the female anatomy grew. I found pornographic magazines hidden in our garage, and I would sneak out there to look at them as often as I could, gazing at the nakedness of women.

When I was 14, I found my dad's 8mm reel movie projector with porn movies. This is where my addiction to porn started. This was the first time I saw men and women having sex. I wanted to be "cool," so I showed it to my best friend, Monty. He mentioned that his dad had some that he found. Then I wondered if his dad were doing the same thing to him and his sister. I was too ashamed to ask or bring it up. What would he think? What would he say? Would he laugh? Would he make fun of me? Would he stop being my friend? I remained silent.

Learn from my mistake. Tell your friend, even better yet, tell your friend's parent. If you are a parent, and you have concerns about what's going on in the lives of your children's friends, please ask them. It may be awkward, but you could be saving a child from continual abuse. Report it if you know that something is going on and the kid is obviously trying to cover up for their family.

For me on the outside, I was your average happy-go-lucky kid. You would have never guessed that I was abused. That's what I wanted you to see. So, don't turn a blind eye to the clues that you may come across. It can be the subtle nudges of God to get you to help get those kids free from their abuser. If something doesn't seem right, check it out. Don't be afraid to ask questions and report it.

Drive-in with my Sisters

My sisters and I loved going to the drive-in. It usually meant we were going to see two movies. We had asked our dad to take us because our mom was traveling to see our grandparents in Germany.

Thinking back on this now, I know that the enemy had a sexual perversion grip on my dad's life. The majority of the memories I have of my father are with him drinking alcohol. One was when my dad took my sisters and me to the drive-in movie. We went to see a double feature of "*Bébé's Kids*" and "*Who Framed Roger Rabbit?*"

My father drank as we enjoyed the movies. After the second movie ended, we left the drive-in parking lot and started heading home. Ten minutes into the drive my father pulled onto the shoulder of an exit ramp and told us we were out of gas. I must have been 12 or 13 at the time, my older sister 13 or 14, and my little sister 9 or 10.

My father announced, "*The only way that I'll go and get some gas is if Kathy gives me what I want.*" I looked over at my older sister, and she was on the verge of tears.

I knew what our father was referring to. So, I said, "*Well, then I'll go and get some gas.*"

My sisters, not wanting to be alone with our father, got out of the car also. The three of us started walking on the shoulder of the road in the middle of the night to the gas station.

We must have walked a mile up the shoulder of the road when our father pulled up beside us and said, "*Get in the car!*" I am sure he realized that three kids walking in the middle of the night on the side of the road would potentially grab the attention of the highway patrol. Not to mention, the amount of drinking that my father did would have gotten him arrested with a DUI charge. Seething, because his plans were ruined, my dad gripped the steering wheel with both hands and continued our drive home in silence. Interestingly enough he never stopped for gas.

When we got home, we were all scared of my father's drunken state. He had a demonic grin on his face that was unsettling, to say the least. We were all terrified. My mom wasn't home, because she was heading back from her trip to Germany. In our two-story townhouse apartment, the stairs leading to the second level were divided. Halfway up the stairs was a mid-landing and the stairs continued in the opposite direction leading to the 2nd story.

The first set of stairs had an open space underneath it creating a triangular gap against the wall that was used for storage. This section of the stairs didn't have backing for each step. Consequently, when you walked up to the stairs, you could see through to the storage area. My mom had put a couch on the side of the stairs making the opened storage access point less conspicuous.

When we got home from the drive-in, we got underneath those stairs and barricaded ourselves from our father. We knew our father was drunk and he wanted one of us. He knew we were there hiding from him. We cried and cried as he mocked us and tried to grab us through space in the stairs. We kept telling him, "*We're going to tell mommy!*"

He retorted back, "*What are you going to tell her? I didn't do anything to you!*"

"*You're trying to hurt us!*" we contested.

He laughed, saying, "*I'm not going to hurt you, will I Kathy?*"

My older sister, already hysterical, shouted, "*Leave us alone!*"

We stayed there together all night. My father finally relented and went upstairs to bed.

The next day my mom was due to be home from her trip. I don't know if my sisters told my mom. All I know is that I didn't. Nothing changed. My father remained in the home. I had no idea the impact that this event had on my life.

It wasn't until later when I went to another counseling session to understand why I had such a hard time protecting anyone but myself. I would like to share this counseling experience with you that took place 23 years after the actual traumatic event. This Christian counseling session called *Sozo* took place in Redding, CA. It was similar to the previous session with my *Restoring the Foundations* counselor. This counselor walked me through similar questions and prayers. When I closed my eyes to allow the Holy Spirit to take me to the hurt that needed truth spoken into, He brought me to this event. "*What do you see?*" the counselor asked.

"I see a toy shield," I said.

The counselor asked, *"Do you want to ask the Holy Spirit why He is showing you this?"*

"Holy Spirit, why are you showing me this?" I asked.

Holy Spirit answered, *"This is the shield that you have placed up as a protective measure. To guard against the attack of the enemy because you felt like it was up to you protect yourself."*

"What do you see now?" the counselor asked.

"I see my sisters and I riding home in the car from the drive-in, and my dad pulled over to say that we are out gas. I hear a voice telling me to get out of the car. It's Jesus!"

I get out of the car, and He motions for my sisters to get out as well.

"Jesus is walking alongside us on the road," I said.

"That's awesome!" the counselor said. *"Is there anything else He's showing you?"*

"Yes, there is a big shield over the stairs of our home and angels standing guard around my sisters and me as we were hiding under the stairs from my father. But this didn't look like my father. This thing had big hideous eyes and was repulsive to look at. It was powerless against

the shield and the angels. The creature went away as soon as it saw the angels." I said.

"Wow!" the counselor exclaimed. *"Holy Spirit was showing you that Jesus and His angels were there protecting you and your sisters. Now you know that He was always with and will always be with you. You can trust Him. There's no need for a toy shield anymore."*

Jeremiah 1:8: *"Do not be afraid of their faces for I am with you, says the Lord."*

Isaiah 41:10: *"Fear not, for I am with you; Be not dismayed, for I am your God. I will strengthen you, Yes, I will help you, I will uphold you with My righteous right hand."*

Seek freedom! I cannot stress enough how important it is for everyone to seek out Spirit-filled, Christian counseling or inner healing ministry. My wife and I both know the power of this ministry.

As you continue to read my story, you will see why it's important to seek counseling as soon as possible. Every decision you make is being made through the lens of what you experience in life. Deciding who to trust and who not to trust. This is how stereotypes, racisms, and prejudices are formed. For me, before these last two healing sessions, I had a hard time trusting older men. I had believed the lie that every

father abuses their kids, especially African American
men.

Chapter 4
Effect on my Adolescence

The last two encounters I had with my father happened when I was a teenager.

My family had opted to do a family movie night complete with pizza and popcorn. There were the three of us teens and we each got to select a movie rental. Typically, we decided on which of our movies was going to be played first. This was done by either the combined interest of the movie or by who fell asleep first. My movie got chosen last because they all knew I was usually the last one up.

Later in the evening, exhausted from being up from watching all three movies, I found myself nodding off during the closing credits of my movie. My sisters and mom had gone upstairs to go to bed after the first two movies. My father nudged me and said, "*Bedtime, dude,*" and left the family room to relieve himself in the downstairs bathroom. I started to get up from the floor, but being tired, I slumped the top half of my body on the couch and my knees remained on the carpet. I started to drift back to sleep. My dad returned to the family room and found me in this position. I wake up to him touching me. My eyes spring open in shock, and I freeze in fear. He pulls my pants down and the unthinkable happens.

When it was over, tears from the pain came down my face. Shame entered me along with guilt. My father threw down a wad of cash next to my face — a gesture to buy my silence. What had I just allowed to happen? I felt dirty. I felt disgusted. I felt ashamed. I felt guilty. Did this mean I was gay?

The next day I remember getting up for Saturday morning cartoons. My older sister was already up watching the movies she missed. I was thankful my father wasn't awake; I did not want to see him. I knew if I saw him, it would remind me of last night along with the shame, guilt, and disgust that I was trying to bury. I just wanted to go outside and play with my friends. I hated being in the house. Being with my friends became an escape from dealing with the pain.

My best friend, Monty, and I had become great friends. We looked alike; we had similar thoughts and interests. Monty introduced me to the world of Marvel and DC Comics. They were still predominantly trading cards and magazines in the '90s. Monty had amassed a great collection of comic cards that I envied. We would talk for hours about epic battles of comic characters.

Being at his house, I had often wondered if Monty were going through what I was going through. Could I be the only one who had a sexually abusive father? His father had been in the Army as well. He and my father looked similar. Later, our fathers became friends. I never built up the courage to ask Monty or tell him what was going on. I was afraid he would laugh at me or ridicule me. I was too ashamed. I didn't want to lose my best friend. I buried my secret.

I want to say this right now at this moment. If you are experiencing any abuse, physical or sexual from a parent, tell your pastor or your teacher. Your pastor or teacher will help you get this information communicated to the proper authorities, and they will keep you safe. I wish I had known to do this because I could have protected myself and my sisters from being repeatedly abused. I didn't know who to trust. I was scared and ashamed. It was easier for me to forget what happened and move on. Unfortunately, this became my mode of functionality. You would have never guessed my father sexually abused me.

My sisters didn't know until I told them in my 20's. It was never talked about among the three of us. I was good at hiding my emotions. I never gave what happened to me a second thought after the encounters. As you continue to read my story, you will see the effects it had on my life through the poor decisions I made. I cannot stress this point enough, if you have experienced sexual abuse in your life, you need to get help. You need to tell someone if it is still going on. You may think forgetting it will be easier. I am telling you, that it will affect every decision you make around relationships. At the end of my book, there will be some resources for you and for someone you know who is struggling.

After this last sexual encounter I had with my father, I was convinced he was trying to make me homosexual. I was 13 years old, and we were up late watching *WWF Summer Slam*. He was drinking and smoking as usual. I was intensely watching the much anticipated Undertaker versus Undertaker match. After the match, my father looked at me with a look I had never seen before. He came over to the couch I was sitting on in a low crawl-like manner. He didn't say a word. Keeping his eyes on the T.V., he reached for the top button and zipper of my pants. I froze in terror not knowing what to do. I will spare you the details because, it was too graphic to share. But midway through the encounter, I panicked and quickly ran up the stairs to my room and slammed the door shut and quickly jumped into my bed and got under the covers. Fearful he would come into my room; I got up and locked the door. I heard him stirring about downstairs. Then I heard him heading up the stairs. I was relieved he didn't come to my door but went into his bedroom.

"Why didn't I run to my mom?" I thought. She was in her room. She could have protected me. What just happened? How do I tell anyone what happened? Was this my fault? Did I allow this to happen? But, I didn't want it to. Why did this happen to me? After wrestling with all of these thoughts, the fear of being told what happened was somehow my fault kept me silent. So, I never told anyone. I buried it.

Please, if you have read this and you need to report sexual abuse that happened to you, but you feel like it was somehow your fault, report it! It wasn't your fault! The truth is the person took advantage of your ability to become sexually stimulated and used it to engage with you sexually. Then when your body responded the way it was designed to, you felt guilty. This is abuse, and you can be free from that guilt and shame.

From what I experienced, I can understand why some men are convinced they are gay and they are born that way. I believe when the "sexually stimulated" door opens, it leaves a lasting impression of what arouses an individual. I believe the enemy plans to pervert and confuse sex in the minds of men and women at really young ages. If the enemy can get you aroused by the same sex early enough, and not understand why your body responded positively, then you can be convinced that you have same-sex attractions. The truth of the matter is that we all can be aroused and that it is God-given, but it is meant to be enjoyed in the context of a heterosexual marriage.

Being aroused doesn't have to come from another person. We can arouse ourselves. However, this is still manipulation, which is not of God.

Ultimately the enemy used my father's struggle with sexual perversion and lust to destroy our relationship and distort my view of the heavenly Father.

The enemy knew if I couldn't trust my earthly father, then I would never trust my Heavenly Father. Do you see how the enemy has so many men or women confused about their sexual preference and identity?

If I were a betting man, I would say the same would be true for women. For women, if a trusted man rapes or abuses them at a young age, a whole host of issues can come flooding in. Especially if that perpetrator is her father, who is supposed to be her protector. When that trust is broken, who can she turn to? What man is she going to trust? This then, opens the door for this woman to seek protection elsewhere. So, when her girlfriends start defending and protecting her from flirting boys, it makes her feel safe. After deciding that intercourse with a man would be a painful reminder of her father, she considers being intimate with a woman. All because her father betrayed and violated her trust.

Let's match her curiosity and safety of women with a willing partner. I'm not saying that all women who are abused by their father will fall into this pattern. All will have trust issues, commitment issues, and have a hard time believing their Heavenly Father loves them and won't abuse them. This mindset, if not resolved, will leave them hard pressed trusting any man, let alone submitting to the lordship of Jesus and making Him their savior.

I hope you are seeing the enemy's tactic in distorting the view of our heavenly Father through horrible experiences. If the enemy can plant a seed of doubt in our minds about our parental security and trust, that seed can mature into a life led by careless decisions, because, now, there is no authority to be trusted, let alone God's. The end goal of Satan, our enemy, is to cause us to hate our loving Creator, by getting us to blame GOD for not protecting us from tragic events. We assume if He didn't protect us, then He must not care or not exist.

Even with this following example, you can see the ethos of this unhealthy belief developing. I was aroused by the same sex, so I must be a homosexual. If it wasn't supposed to happen, where was God to

33

protect me? This is not true. You were aroused by a sensation given by God that was meant to be revealed and activated on your wedding night by an opposite-sex spouse. Because this was awakened and manipulated early in your childhood by the wrong person, you are convinced you're homosexual. I'll say it again - this is the biggest scheme of the enemy. I had to allow God to break this belief in me by showing me my first sexual encounter.

If you are struggling, just know what happened to you in your childhood wasn't your fault. You were abused and taken advantage of. There is hope for you. You can be restored. I had a distorted view of God the Father. When my wife or someone said, "You just need to get into God's lap and be intimate with Him," you can only imagine the type of thoughts that would come into my mind. Especially when the Bible refers to Christians as the Bride of Christ! The following thought would plague my mind: *So if I'm Jesus' Bride, does that mean what I think it means?*" That thought in and of itself was a seed of doubt. I highly encourage you to seek out freedom ministry and run after the healing that Jesus offers!

Chapter 5
Girlfriends

When I was 17, I had my first sexual encounter with a girl other than my sister. Glenda was a freshman and I was a junior. I knew she had a huge crush on me. I took advantage of that.

One day, I offered to drive Glenda home from school. She gladly accepted. We arrived at her empty house. She invited me in. We talked, and I convinced her that I wanted her though I was secretly dating another freshman who wasn't supposed to date until she was 17. I knew Glenda was infatuated with me; I went for it and kissed her. I asked if she ever had sex. She said, "No, not yet." With that flirtatious reply, I knew she would do anything to be with me. So, we did it without protection. The moment after I climaxed, I felt fear. I was scared I had gotten her pregnant. She looked at me with the same fear.

We were blinded - me wanting to satisfy my sexual lust, and Glenda wanting to feel desired and special and hoping to gain it by trading her special treasure for it. But what we both felt seconds after sex was <u>fear</u>. I'm sure Glenda felt fear because her parents were going to kill her for getting pregnant. She voiced, *"My parents told me if I ever got pregnant they were going to send me to live with my aunt in Mexico!"* I felt fear because I wasn't ready to bring another life into this world. I reassured her we'd be okay and get through this together.

I was late for work. At 17, I had a job drying cars at a carwash. I knew making minimum wage would never support a child. I asked coworkers to get some insight and options of what to do. The thought of being a father dominated my thinking, I was seriously worried. I selfishly imagined being stuck in my hometown and never living out my dreams. One guy said you should get her the morning after pill and that should take care of it. So, I looked into it. By the time I could get Glenda to a clinic, it would have been five days. So, we just waited it out.

I begged and pleaded to God that Glenda would not get pregnant. Three days later, my prayer was answered, and Glenda got her period. I had never been more thankful for a woman's menstrual cycle. I didn't learn my lesson. I bought condoms. We had sex every day I saw her. When she was on her period, she did other things to satisfy my sexual lust. Glenda wanted to know she had my attention, and she did all she could to keep it.

This was a bad combination, my lust, and growing sex addiction mixed with her low self-esteem, low self-worth, and need to be validated.

I remember cutting school one day just to take Glenda to my house to have sex. My mom came home for lunch that day. Glenda and I panicked in my bedroom as I heard my mom coming up the stairs. I told Glenda to get in my closet. She complied, and as she shut the door, my mom opened my bedroom door. My mom asked, *"Son, what are you doing home?"* Quick on my feet, I responded with, *"I had some time between classes* (I was a senior, and I had four classes each day), *and I wanted to come home to do some homework and workout. That's why my shirt was off."* *"Well, why don't you come downstairs and have lunch with me?"* my mom asked, *"Okay, I'll be down in a minute,"* I said. As soon as my mom made her way down the stairs, I went to my closet and told Glenda to stay in the closet and not move. I knew the creaking sound of the floorboards would tip off my mom that someone was in my bedroom.

As I went downstairs to have lunch with my mom, Glenda waited quietly for thirty minutes in my cluttered and tiny closet until my mom left. Glenda was furious but relieved we didn't get caught. God was trying to get my attention. He warned me with the pregnancy scare. Now, He was warning me with almost getting caught.

God, our heavenly Father, tries to warn us in subtle ways. Jentezen Franklin explained it in his sermon titled "Ministry of the Moth." God will first send a moth to tickle your ear to get your attention about a matter. The moth being persistent will keep trying to get your attention until you shoo it away enough. Then God will use more aggressive methods that will grab your attention. Jentezen Franklin then shared a story of a mother who repeatedly told her child to look both ways before crossing the street. One day, her child wasn't paying attention as usual and started crossing a street. The mother saw her child about to cross the street and noticed a car coming on the road nearing her non-attentive child. She sprints to her child. Clenching down on her child's bare arm and pulling with all of her strength in the opposite direction of the threatening vehicle, she saved his life. But her child now bears a bloody arm. A wound from the indentations of his mother's nails where she grabbed him and pulled him to safety. Forever scarred with the memory of the close call with death. Finally, he has learned to look both ways before crossing the street. God will use anything He can to keep you from going to hell. He doesn't want you to die in your sin. Even if He has to put you in prison, He'll do it. He'd rather have you in prison allowing you to give your sin to Him than for you to die and go to hell because of your sin.

2 Peter 3:9 (NLT): *"The Lord isn't really being slow about his promise, as some people think. No, he is being patient for your sake. He does not want anyone to be destroyed but wants everyone to repent."*

However, the scare of getting caught doesn't keep me from having sex. I had shooed away the moth. It was exciting and thrilling to not get caught. It got to the point where we would do it hiding in her backyard while her parents were home. My lust drove me. I became a slave to it. I was chasing the feeling that came with the release of endorphins in my brain. It was an addiction. I didn't care how I got the release. When I needed to have another hit of endorphins, I masturbated.

Glenda asked me what I wanted for my birthday, and I told her that she already knew. Later, when she found out I was joining the Navy, she was devastated. She knew for sure I would dump her. I assured her that I would marry her after she graduated, and we'd live happily ever after. I gave her a promise ring in the fall of 2000 to seal my intentions with her.

When I left for Military Entrance Processing Station (MEPS) in Sacramento, my mom, sisters, and Glenda cried, but I remained dry-eyed. I was excited to leave my home. It reminded me of the pain and shame I had endured and now I felt as if I was finally going to be free.... so, I thought.

Later, that afternoon I arrived at the hotel and checked into my room. The guy who was sharing the hotel room with me was leaving for boot camp the same day I was. I suggested we go down to the pool and check out the girls. In short, because the lust was so strong in me, I cheated on my girlfriend the same day I left her. I had no remorse or intention of remaining faithful to her. Lust kept me from feeling the hurt I was causing people. I was too prideful and selfish to care for anyone else.

The next day I went through my physical, and I got shipped off to Great Lakes, Illinois for boot camp.

When I completed boot camp two months later, I sent money to Glenda for a plane ticket to come along with my family to my Pass and Review (graduation). I was so glad to see her.

Our Recruit Drill Commanders (RDC), better known as "Drill Sergeants," told us while we were out on liberty to be with our families that we weren't allowed to show any public display of affection (PDA) while in uniform. If we were caught, we would have to do boot camp all over again. If we decided to take an extra day that was unauthorized and not report in for our assigned duty day for the weekend, we would bear the same consequences of repeating boot camp. They scared us pretty good. So much so that Glenda noticed that change in me. I wouldn't hold her hand let alone kiss her in public.

Glenda felt that I was pushing her away. All she wanted to do was to kiss and embrace me. I told her we had to do that later out of the public eye. I was so intimidated by the RDC's command that I didn't embrace any of my family members in public. I was sure they all thought I was brainwashed. The RDC's said they would be out in town in plain clothes watching. They had plenty of military personnel in town who would inform them of violators to their command; I didn't want to chance it.

However, Glenda lied to her parents about the graduation length. She told them it would be three days versus two, so we could have our private time in the hotel once my family left. What she didn't anticipate was the guy who lived on the edge had been scared straight. I knew, if I had left the base the third day without a leave pass to return with, I was going to be repeating boot camp. Not an option! Alternatively, Glenda stayed on the base with me, and I dared not to try to seek a thrill.

If the command is clear enough, and the consequences detrimental enough, we as humans are more likely to obey. I knew I would die if I had to repeat boot camp.

Adam and Eve obeyed God initially. After all, the consequence was death. So, let's go back to Eden and see what transpired.

Yes, initially they were obedient to God by not eating the forbidden fruit. Adam and Eve didn't want to die. But, how does that sound to you? As long as you do what I say, you won't die. Coming from a God that has given you the literal world to rule, given you plenty of food to eat, and has only one rule to follow. I would say that's a pretty good deal, wouldn't you? However, God's test wasn't complete.

A perfect and all-knowing God doesn't want robots. God is love. It is His very fiber and being. He loves us more than we can ever understand. He gave Adam and Eve a love lesson. Since love is built on trust, God gave them a test to see if they would obey Him. This is not because God is insecure. It was necessary because if all Adam and Eve knew was good and never had the opportunity to disobey and not trust Him, then God knows that he created robots. They had no other choice, which meant that true love could not exist. Adam and Eve were programmed to do only one function: to do what God said.

This is not loving but programming. Think about your computer's keyboard. It is programmed to do what you want. When you push the "X" key, it produces an "X." It has no choice but to execute your command. It doesn't type an "X" because you loved it or that it loved you. It typed an "X" because, it was programmed that way. Without another choice to make, we would all be "X's" doing what God told us to do. God is not a dictator; we can all look back through history and identify dictators.

Forceful, aggressive, controlling, oppressive leaders who have tried to make or command people to do certain things to exert their authority over them. This is very different from what God was doing in Eden.

He needed to see if they would still follow Him out of obedience and trust. Trust was being established between God and His created beings. Without obedience, there is no trust; and without trust, there is no love. God entrusted Adam and Eve with the whole Earth to rule and reign over. Now comes the test of trust for Adam and Eve. Will they obey God's one commandment and trust that God has their best interest in mind? Sadly, we know the answer to our creation story.

Friends, we all have disobeyed God because we think that he was trying to keep something from us. Rest assured we serve a forgiving God; all we have to do is ask for forgiveness for violating His laws, accept His son's sacrifice for the purchase of our sins and make Him the LORD of our life.

The great thing about Jesus' blood it's not only covering our shame, guilt, and sins, but it washes us white as snow making us appear though we never committed those things. You were created for a unique purpose in this world. When you partner with God, you can live out those purposes. God covers you.

He has been wooing you all this time. I know this because he was wooing me when I didn't realize it - even when I was seeking validation elsewhere.

Chapter 6
Validation by Drinking

Once I got to my "A" School, the next step of a seaman's naval career, all the brainwashing for reverence to the higher-ranking petty officers vanished in one check-in process at this school.

The petty officer first class who checked me in was so disdained by the proper title of Petty Officer. When he asked me where I was from, I responded standing at attention "*I'm from California, Petty Officer.*"

He quickly retorted and said, "*Don't call me that S&*!, My name is OS1 Smith.*"

I quickly respond with, "*Aye-aye Petty Officer.*"

He looked me over and said, "*You gotta lose that boot camp BS if you want to stay at my school. It's OS1, you got that?*"

"*Yes, sir, I mean OS1,*" I responded, correcting myself.

"*Don't you dare call me, 'sir'. I work for a living!*"

I looked blankly at the overweight man not knowing how to respond. OS1 Smith, went back to the check-in process, telling me all I needed to know about what I would be doing before I classed up, where I would be sleeping, when the hours of the chow hall were opened if I chose to eat there, and the liberty (free time) that I had. It was a night and day difference between boot camp and "A" school.

After getting to know some of the guys in my class, we started venturing out. We had to wear our uniform when we went out on liberty for the first four weeks of school. Not that we had much of an option. The only civilian clothes that we had were the ones we wore to boot camp. Most of us couldn't get to the mall because we had no wheels. So, we had to quickly make friends with those who had cars. After making friends with some classmates who were local to the area, I got to venture out. I wanted to fit in with the boys. Checking out women was on every young sailor's mind as well as drinking. Most of these guys I hung around with were my age, fresh out of high school. I knew none of them were at the legal drinking age, but, that didn't keep them from finding places that served alcohol to under-aged sailors. Most of these places said things like, 'if you're old enough to sacrifice your life, you should be old enough to drink.'

I never had gotten drunk before. Sure, I snuck a drink from my mom's wine cooler before and tasted my dad's beer but nothing to the point of feeling drunk. Sitting down with these guys and contributing money for pitchers and pitchers of beer, I felt obligated to drink. I was trying to be like one of the guys. I hated the taste of beer and still do. Yet, I drank it, mug after mug trying to earn validation from my peers. After the third beer, I had to get up to relieve myself. But when I stood up, I felt the room shift. My brain was buzzing. My face started to get numb. Stumbling into the bathroom I had to focus, so I wouldn't pee on my shoes. I got back to the table, and one of the guys had ordered a round of shots. Of course, I said I was game. I wanted these guys to like me. I needed friends. I needed to prove that I belonged there. I was looking for validation. I don't remember the rest of the night. The next thing I remembered was lying down on my top bunk and the room would not stop spinning. Even when I closed my eyes, I felt myself spin in my bed. I was miserably drunk.

I never wanted to feel that way again. But, if I wanted these guys to be my friends, I had to make that sacrifice.

Thankfully I had other ambitions. I wanted to get orders to Pearl Harbor, Hawaii. I knew when we graduated school we got to pick our own orders. The tradition was to rank students by how well they performed in

47

their class. That ranking determined the order in which the sailors got to pick from the available duty station billets. So, I focused on my schoolwork and got away from distractions, like class clowns and late night drinking parties. I studied most nights. My goal was to rank as close to the top of the 40 sailors in my class as possible. At graduation, I finished 7th in my class. There were only three billets to Hawaii. I was sure everybody wanted to go there.

To my surprise, the first two orders selected were to Keflavik, Iceland. The hook was automatic promotion to Petty Officer third class. The next person went up to the board and grabbed Virginia. He was from there and wanted to stay close to home. My study buddy grabbed Hawaii. I was in shock! He told me he would likely pick a billet closer to home in Virginia. Two Hawaii billets remained on the board. I was third away from picking. I didn't have a backup pick. It was either going to be orders to Hawaii or I was going to be miserable. The next person picked Florida. Whew. I knew it was in the bag now. All I had to do was walk up to the board and select Hawaii when my turn came. And I did! My hard work paid off.

I learned something about myself that day. If I put my mind to something and really focus on accomplishing it, by removing all distractions, I can achieve it. Hard work and determination really do pay off. I believe the Holy Spirit was guiding me to make the right decisions that would help obtain the desires of my heart. Even though, I wasn't acknowledging Him nor seeking Him.

Chapter 7
Lust is an Insatiable Beast

Let me get right to the truth of the matter. Lust is a demon, an evil spirit whose hunger can never be satisfied. Once you allow this evil spirit access to you, it will want nothing less than your life. It will consume your every thought, your every resource, anything and everything you find joy. You will be twisted, manipulated, and perverted to feed his insatiable appetite. It's goal and very existence is to destroy you, your family, and your generation. Yes, it wants to solidify its effect of sexual perversion in your future generation. It wants to continue to move from this generation to the next. How do I know this? Up to this point, I've been sharing stories about how my father molested me in my childhood and adolescence. Now, you're going to read about how this spirit of lust lived on through my life. Later, you will read how God was able to break that cyclic grip of the spirit of lust and perversion off my family's future generations.

When I was at Pearl Harbor, Hawaii, my first duty station, the spirit of lust was strong on me. I remember times when the guys and I would go into the town of Waikiki and look for a good time which typically meant checking out women. The beaches would never be empty of women scantily dressed in bikinis tanning themselves on the beautiful shores of Hawaii.

This was paradise. It was a playground for sexually charged lustful men looking to have a good time. We were getting glimpses of the female anatomy that was usually covered up anywhere else. Since I was visually stimulated, it didn't take much for my brain to start thinking about sex. After overdosing on half dressed women all day, I'd go home with my new collection of mental pictures and masturbate. I thought about sex all the time. While I was standing duty or driving my car, any dead space void of thinking was set to the default of thinking about sex. I'd replay from my memory what a woman's butt looked like at the gym and imagine seeing it nude and having sex with it.

Did you catch that? I referred to having sex with it and not her. Women were only valuable in my eyes to the body part they carried. Yes, I viewed women as carriers of the sex organs for my sexual gratification. They were objects for my sexual pleasure, not people. I gained an addiction to looking at women — staring at them, checking out their bodies, imagining sexual positions with them.

My mind was constantly on this track of thinking about every woman I found remotely attractive. My mind, overrun with lust, was addicted to sex. This lust spirit that was living in me was always hungry. And at that time in my life, I was enjoying it. I wasn't hurting anybody. I was single and enjoying myself. Poor insecure and selfish me. Later in my life I would find out how much I was hurting myself, my future wife and family. I spent many years in this lustful way of thinking. I had no idea that it was bad or wrong. After all, didn't every man think this way? I understood that my dad did. The guys I hung around did. It was virtually accepted by every male I knew in my life. This way of thinking dominated my teenage and young adult life. Even when I had girlfriends, my eyes would wander to check out every passing female. Most of my girlfriends didn't like it. Some didn't say anything; they would just end the relationship. I didn't care. I was in those relationships for the sex. I did what I had to do to satisfy the lust monster living inside of me. The girlfriends who didn't like me looking at other girls caused me to adjust my approach. I wouldn't look at another woman directly; I would wait to catch a glimpse in a reflection, or I would wear sunglasses. I needed to feed my lust dog. I had to look. I needed to see. I needed mental pictures. My mind was addicted, and I had to see the female anatomy so that my lustful fantasies could be lived out in the mind.

Understand, my friends, I was addicted to looking. I was addicted to lustful fantasies. It was consuming me. I was feeding it multiple times a day, every day. When women in bikinis weren't available, then I checked out the women at the mall. When I couldn't watch a pornographic movie, then I would watch movies that had sex scenes or women dressed in revealing clothing. When I was stuck in the middle of the ocean standing watch on an all-male ship or stuck in traffic driving to work, I had my mental picture album to fall back on. I had so much stored imagery in my brain that I could recall any porn that I watched or woman in a bikini or any sexual encounter I had with a girl. It was all there. My lustful desires could feast on this for hours to the point of masturbation. The interesting thing was my mind memory was never full; it could always take on new images. It was the perfect storage device for the spirit of lust.

What you feed will live, and what you starve will die.

Don't feed the black dog. This is something Winston Churchill said when referring to his battle with depression. In his battle of hopelessness and despair during the advancement of the Nazi war machine, he knew when he gave his thoughts over to hopelessness and despair; he was feeding depression a steak dinner.

When his thoughts of giving up tried to overrun his mind which were substantiated with no real solutions, he would resist. Churchill would think of positive solutions and ask positive questions that could produce positive and favorable results. Conversely, he would never ask negative questions. Churchill would always phrase them in a positive frame. For example, he wouldn't ask *"Why can't I come up with a solution to defeat the Nazi regime?"* Instead, he would ask, *"How can I defeat the Nazi regime?"* The first question is asking the question in a defeated posture which feeds the black dog of depression. *"Why can't I?"* equals despair and defeat.

The second question asks *"How can I?"* which encourages positive thought that will lead to a solution yet discovered. Do you hear the difference in the question? This is a mere example of the importance of asking good questions. Good questions lead to favorable solutions.

So, men, as we try to figure out why we struggle with our thoughts and how to overcome them, we first need to ask a question that will give us the favorable result we are hoping to obtain. How can I overcome the thoughts that are running through my mind? Let's think through the example of Winston Churchill and see if we can apply what he did to overcome depression.

We have to stop feeding the spirit of lust. Once we start feeding this spirit, it can never ever be satisfied. After it has consumed us, it will move on to our children and live on throughout our generations until someone closes the door that was opened. The open door is giving rightful passage for evil spirits to oppress us. You might ask, "*Why would anyone in their right mind, willingly open the door for an evil spirit?*" Well, unfortunately, we do it all the time, knowingly or unknowingly. More often than not, it's unknowingly. More accurately stated it's ignorantly opened.

I believe we all have this innate sense of what right and wrong is. We get that from Adam and Eve. Here is what I did to help stop feeding the spirit of lust. This is not an exhaustive list, nor is it the only thing you need to do. Let me say this so that it is clear as well. <u>Nothing that is done apart from GOD will ever work</u>.

For it is not by our works that set us free, it is the power of the blood of Jesus Christ that sets us free. Jesus is the one who paid with His life for all the wrong and evil we did to violate God's law. Death was the only acceptable form of payment for sin. Because Jesus lived a perfect life without sin, hell and death had to refund Jesus' payment back to God the Father. Now anybody who believes Jesus Christ died for them on that cross, taking their place, can use the same form of payment towards their sin and know that in their death they will be refunded back to God the Father. Hallelujah!

First, you have to **repent of your sin**. Make Jesus your Lord and Savior. Once you have done that with all sincerity in your heart, then the Holy Spirit can begin working on the inside of you. You have to yield to His voice. The Holy Spirit will begin to show you what you need to get rid of in your life. These are things and thoughts that are not honoring to God or your temple. Your body is your temple where the Holy Spirit lives.

Read 1 Corinthians 6:19-20. Do you remember in the Bible where Jesus went into the temple of God and flipped tables over chasing away all the money changers and whipping them saying, "*This is to be a house of prayer, stop making my Father's temple a den of thieves?*" Read it in Matt 21: 12. This is what the Holy Spirit will do with you. He will cleanse your mind and renew it, but you have to be yielded to Him, so the renewing of your mind can happen.

At the end of my book, I will share with you what the Holy Spirit showed me what I needed to get rid of and what to do to keep my temple holy. I didn't fully understand the consequences of the decisions and choices I was making and the effects it had on me.

Let's go back to Adam and Eve eating from the tree of the knowledge of good and evil. They didn't fully comprehend the consequences of eating that forbidden fruit. Sure, they were told they would die and that should be conclusive in and of itself, but they were led to believe that God was keeping something from them. Does having opposition to God's word justify their disobedience? After all, Adam and Eve didn't drop dead after they ate the forbidden fruit. Was God keeping this from them as the serpent suggested? No, of course not, but the opposition was needed to secure the possibility of trust which is the seed of love.

Adam and Eve did die 900 years later.

I often wonder if God's original plan was for humans to live forever. I believe so, because after this incident, Adam and Eve were kicked out of the Garden so they wouldn't eat from the tree of life. I believe if Adam and Eve had remained loyal to God's commandment, the reward would have been granted to eat from the tree of life. Rev 22:14. Their love and trust for God were put to the test. Did they truly believe God was keeping them from dying or was this new and opposing information revealing that God was holding something back?

More often than not people have this bent towards God. Is God holding back something from me?

Why can't I win the lottery? Why can't I have sex before marriage? Why can't I live with my girlfriend? Why can't I do these drugs? Why can't I masturbate? Why can't I...? You fill in the blank. All these questions are rooted in a self-centered understanding of what we think will make our lives better, or make us feel better, or gives us freedom of choice.

From what I have experienced, I was never correct in my own thinking or assumptions of what I thought were good for me.

"Do not be wise in your own eyes; fear the Lord and depart from evil." Proverbs 3:7

Satan will always come at us with lies mixed with half-truths so we can justify doing what we know is contrary to God's word. *"There is a way that seems right to man, but its end is the way of death."* Proverbs 14:12.

Sex does give you pleasure. God created it, but God created it to be more than physical pleasure. It was created to be the most intimate and special union a man and woman can enjoy together.

This exclusive gift was to be coveted and experienced with your spouse. It is to be the representation of God and man coming so close in their relationship that they have become one operating in power fueled by the pleasure of working in unison. Gen 2:24, 1 Sam 10:6, Mark 10:7-9, Luke 1:35, Acts 1:8

59

But when we seek after the physical pleasure and forsake the marital relationship, sex will never satisfy you the way it was created. In fact, you will feel like there was something missing and wrong or even dirty and used. Sex without the committed covenant of a biblical marriage is like having apples when you could be having apple pie.

Women, let me interject something here to help us men to starve this lustful spirit. First, let me ask you some questions. If you met a man and you knew he was in bondage to a spirit of lust, would you date him? What type of man are you looking for? What do you want him to appreciate the most about you? What do you want him to admire about you? If you want to be pursued by a man with good character and moral values governed by a heart led by Christ, then use the bait that will attract him.

Mainly your character and confidence in who you are. If you dress in a way that attracts a type of man who is attracted to your bodily features, then you caught what you were fishing for. Don't be surprised if that man wants to jump into bed with you and later looks at other women the same way he looked at you. His heart is filled with lust. He has an insatiable appetite that will never be quenched by you. This is how I looked at women. If a woman was flaunting what she had or dressed in a certain way, she was the type of woman I was after.

She had the same mindset I had; in short, let's hook up and move on. If that's not what you want in a man, and you're seeking a man who will care for you and love you and forsake all others, then you need to fish with the right bait. When you dress, highlight the areas you want to be known and appreciated for.

Cover up the rest and reveal them to your husband on your wedding night. Present it to him as a gift. Share it with the one whom you've entrusted your all to. Don't buy into the lie, "If you got it, flaunt it!" Don't cheapen your merchandise. Treat it as it is, highly expensive. Only one man should get to see and know all of you.

If you have given away that special treasure, immediately put it under lock and key. If your boyfriend doesn't value your choice of not having sex anymore until you're married, then he is not the man for you. A man should value women and not treat them as sexual objects.

You are a daughter of God. You are very expensive. Your worth is far more valuable than the cheap thrills of sex. You were made to be loved, cherished, adored, and protected. You were not meant to be taken advantage of.

Again, I say to you ladies, put your treasure under lock and key. Re-evaluate the man you are dating and set your standards of what type of man you want. Ask yourself, "Is the way I'm dressing attracting a man who only wants sex or the man I don't want?" Never settle for a man you don't want because you're tired of being alone. Enjoy your singleness. Once you get married and have some kids, you'll have to think with all of them in mind, which means you will have to make some sacrifices for the betterment of your new family. Go travel and see some places, finish school, do the things that you enjoy doing. The perfect man will come along when it's time.

Chapter 8
Falling in Lust and Duped into Marriage

I met an attractive woman on the streets of Hawaii. I was too nervous to say anything to her, and my friends wanted to keep moving down the Waikiki Strip to the nearby clubs and bars. The woman and I kept stealing glances at each other until she approached me and asked if I knew of any place where she could get some weed. I called my friends back, and we got her connected with what she requested. We exchanged numbers and hung out that night. I was too terrified to do any illicit drugs, so I passed on the numerous offers she gave me to smoke with her. She had some other friends with her. I found out she was traveling with her friend's family on vacation. Over the next few days, we connected and hooked up. We talked a lot about sex, porn, and drinking. She got so wasted the last night we were together she blurted out and said, "I want to marry you" We laughed it off. Hindsight tells me that should have been a red flag, but it wasn't.

We stayed in touch over the phone for the next couple of months. I invited her to a huge birthday bash my friend and I were throwing since our birthdays were a day apart. My friend's childhood friend's dad was a retired officer, and through him, we were able to score a beach house for our drink fest birthday bash. She wanted to come but couldn't afford a ticket to come. So, I bought Jane a ticket mainly to have a guaranteed hook up. I picked Jane up from the airport and took her to the beach house. She gave me porn as a present for my birthday. I was in love with this girl. She knew how to play on my lust. If I were to marry any girl, Jane would be it. She wanted sex more than I did, and she bought me porn. Later that evening with so much alcohol and so many people there at the beach house, it became the ultimate party scene. Some of the other girls that were invited to the party came and found me. They wanted to hook up, so we got to talking. Jane found me and was pissed. After much convincing and apologizing, she calmed down and took me to the bedroom, and we had sex.

A couple of weeks passed by. Jane and I stayed connected over the phone because she lived in California. On a particular conversation, Jane began to ask me questions about integrity and family. She asked, *"If a friend of yours got a girl pregnant, what would you tell your friend to do?"*

I responded something like, "*Well I would suggest that he marry the girl to make it right, that the kid needs a father.*" (This comes from seeing my older sister struggle not having her baby's daddy there and support their son).

That's when Jane told me she was 36 days pregnant with twins. (Red flag alert!) I was in shock; but I said, "*Are you sure and can you send me proof?*" After about a week, she emailed me a picture of a sonogram. After the evidence, I said, "*Well, we should get married.*" I had to eat my words, but it was fine because this was the sex loving, porn giving gal that I could see myself marrying. I told her that we would get married after I got back from the six-month deployment that I was leaving for in two months. Jane insisted we get it done before I left so she could get settled in Hawaii and have what she needed during the pregnancy.

So, I told my mom the story about Jane, obviously leaving out the drunken party, illicit drugs, and porn. I remember arrogantly telling my mom that we loved each other and we never argued. Besides, she was 36 days pregnant with my twins. My mom replied with something that really should have carried more weight than it did. She scoffed and said you can't know that early if you're having twins. I sent my mom the sonogram and she said why is her name not on this? I pushed those concerns and doubts to the side. I was blinded by lust. After all, the wedding plans were set.

Three days before I was due to arrive in San Diego to meet her family, she told me she lost the babies. With a humble tone, she asked, "*You probably don't want to get married now, do you?*" Feeling sorry and full of pride and not wanting to look like a jerk I said, "*Yes, of course, I do*".

We pushed forward with our plans. I flew to San Diego. I spent a week getting to know her mom and stepdad. Jane told me to tell her parents we knew each other from school so it would calm her family's suspicion and concern of rushing into this too quickly. (Something in me wanted to object to these plans, but I went along with it.) Shame and guilt have a way of controlling your thoughts. Jane's biological father came and picked us up for lunch. We told him the same story that we fabricated for her mom. Her father paid for our wedding in Las Vegas. Jane's mom took us to buy our wedding bands. We drove with her mom and stepdad to Las Vegas to get married.

My mom, dad, sisters, and infant nephew came to our wedding. Before we walked down the aisle, my mom pulled me to the side and said, "*Son, are you sure you want to do this?*" I said, "*Sure mom, I love her.*" My mom hesitantly said, "*Okay, my son, I'm happy for you then.*" My dad never said anything to me that I can remember.

I told Jane's parents my dad was a truck driver. Although months prior to the wedding day, his license was taken away for speeding and possession of illicit drugs. It's amazing what pride and shame will do together. It will cover up for people that have hurt you the most when your (false) identity is at risk of being exposed.

The rush of getting everything ready for Jane before I left, had us both stressed. We had to get her a car and an apartment. We had to file military paperwork that would give me an increase in pay to support a new dependent and grant allowance for housing. We got Jane connected with a military spouse's support group that offered support while the military member was deployed. Jane made some friends with my friends' girlfriends. They had met at the birthday bash. It was amazing what we accomplished in 60 days. We got married, got a new car, an apartment, furniture, financial support, and military family support. Just in time before we had to say our goodbyes.

The South Pacific Deployment Infidelity

While on deployment, I wanted to ensure Jane had all the support she needed. She was completely isolated from her family back in California, and now she was isolated from me. She had made some quick friends with my buddy's girlfriends. They were college students attending the University of Hawaii. They created a common bond of missing their men and partying. I was excited to see the world; this was one of the reasons that I joined the Navy. Our deployment was scheduled for six months to circle the south pacific near the middle and South America to interrupt drug operations.

Our base of operations was Panama. I was excited about this deployment. I loved the Latin culture — the food, the women, mainly the women. Our ship pulled into Guatemala. We had a limited range of liberty which meant that because the country was not stable enough to accommodate us, the country's port authority set up some local vendors to come in with their food and crafted goods to sell to us a few yards from the ship. There was no leaving the gated port; there was no venturing out and exploring the sights of Guatemala. So, I shopped a day amongst the artisans and bought a couple of items for my newlywed wife.

Next stop Costa Rica. What a beautiful place. My friends and I wanted to see this place. We wanted to get as far away from the ship in the authorized liberty zone as possible. We got a cab, and the four of us piled in and told the cabby to take us to the beach with food and take us to a strip club afterward. One of our friends, Frankie, was Dominican and spoke Spanish. So, the cabby took us about an hour away. We crossed a river on a small car ferry. I started to get nervous when we pulled up to a place that looked like the middle of the jungle. I remember asking Frankie," *Dude, where is he taking us? This doesn't look like the beach. There is nothing out here. Do you think this guy is setting us up?*"

We had heard and had been warned by stories of sailors getting ambushed by the locals in different countries. This was the very reason why the military set up safe liberty zones for us to abide by. But we were young and dumb and wanted to live dangerously and look brave in front of friends. It sounded cool to say but when you were doing it, you started to have second thoughts. To our surprise, we pulled up to a restaurant. It looked like a hole in the wall. On the other side of the thick brush was the beach. Wow, what a view! That is when I asked Frankie, "*What does Costa Rica mean in Spanish?*" "*Cost of Riches or Rich Cost.*" It was beautiful. I could see why they called it that. We went inside the restaurant for a meal. The food was amazing!

After spending some time goofing around on that beautiful yet empty beach, we decided to get in the cab and head to our other planned destination.

The destination resembled an abandoned office building. Our cabby, now insisting to be paid and wanting to leave, heightened our awareness of being outside the safe liberty zone. We asked him to pick us up in a few hours to take us back to the ship, but he refused and said that he was done for the day. We made our way into the building concluding we would have to figure out how we were going to get back to the ship later. We walked inside the building. It was lit up with neon lights and thick with cloudy smoke from pipes and cigars. The smell of alcohol and nude women dancing on the stage in sync with the Latin music created a wild and crazy atmosphere. My heart was beating uncontrollably in my chest. Did I not feel safe? Was I nervous? Was this fear? Thoughts of Jane came into my mind. That was it. Did I feel as if I were cheating on Jane, by being here? Would she be hurt that I was here? One of my friends must have been reading the look on my face. He whispered in my ear, *"What happens on deployment stays on deployment!"* My other friend found a table and Frankie ordered us some drinks. My conscience, not wanting to yield with the notion of covering up of the potential events of the night, warned louder, *"She would be hurt you'd do this to her. Remember, when she got upset with you for talking with another girl at your birthday party?"* My flesh protested with, *"She got you the porn for your birthday, didn't she? So obviously, you looking at another nude woman is no big deal and she welcomes it."* So, I sat there drinking away my conscious and allowing my lust to take in the sights of the club.

The next day while on duty on the ship, I got a chance to call Jane. I told her about the deployment, about the restaurant trip, and the Guatemala gift I got her. I didn't tell her about the strip club. Jane told me about some

70

car trouble she had and an incident she had where she felt she was being followed. I told her that I was glad she was okay.

She was quiet for a while. Then I heard sniffles and her voice cracked. *"Tim,"* she began, *"I... kissed another guy."* *"Nothing else happened,* "she quickly reassured. *"I was lonely and the girls and I had some friends over and I kissed this guy."*

My heart sank. Not knowing what to say, I remained quiet.

Jane asked, *"Tim, are you still there? Are you mad at me? Say something?"*

"How could you, Jane!" I said.

"I'm sorry," apologetically responding.

"I don't want you to see this guy again!" I demanded.

"Okay... Do you forgive me?" Jane asked.

My mind flooded with images of her doing more than just kissing this guy. *"Are you sure you didn't do more than that Jane?"*

"Yes, I'm sure," her voice now more defiant.

"I don't believe you, Jane." I protested. *"You had sex with this guy, didn't you!"*

"NO, I promise, I didn't!"

"Please, believe me, I felt so bad about the kiss and if I had, I would tell you. I am just so convicted about this. I just want to be honest with you; don't you want that for our marriage?" Jane asked.

"Well, yeah, I do. But I don't want you around other guys. Do I make myself clear?"

"Yes, you do," Jane replied.

"Well, my time is up here on the phone. I'll call you again soon," I said.

We hung up, and I wrestled with the notion of why I didn't come clean. She told me about kissing another guy. Why couldn't I tell her about the strip club? Was it pride? Did I justify it as being a common thing in our marriage, that it wasn't a big deal since she was the one that bought me porn?

The next time out with the guys I could not get the images of Jane kissing another guy out of my head. I told my good friend about it. He concluded she was probably already shacking up with the guy and I might as well have fun. After a couple of rounds of shots, my friend bought me a prostitute. I'd love to say I felt guilty after cheating on Jane, but I didn't. I felt like I had gotten even. She started it, and I wanted payback. She hurt me and I was going to hurt her. Yet, I didn't quit after one prostitute. I had slept with one in every port that we pulled into on that deployment. Even though I thought I was getting even with Jane, it made me feel empty. I started to feel worse about myself. Here I was taking vengeance into my own hands trying to make me feel better; it was back-firing. I had sunk to a new low of degrading myself. This wasn't doing anything to fix the problem. It was just making it worse. Not only did I think that Jane was cheating on me, I was doing it.

I believe that is why God says in his word that vengeance is His. He knows if we did the avenging, that would make matters worse. I was drinking poison hoping it would affect Jane. The truth is that poison hurt us both. If you suspect your spouse is cheating on you, don't do like I did and take the matter into your own hands. Pray that God would reveal to you the truth and let HIM handle it. God's heart is for reconciliation. He wants to redeem us all. Yes, there should be consequences. Trust will need to be won back. Yes, the road will be long ahead of you. But, if you truly want reconciliation like the Father in heaven does, then trust that He will help you get there.

After getting home from deployment, Jane was so happy to see me. Honestly, I was too. Two weeks after getting home, Jane started developing painful sores. Being newlyweds and naïve, I asked her if she had ever had this type of sore before. She said no. After getting checked out at the clinic, the doctor told us that it was an STD called herpes. I thought of my childhood. I remembered I use to get an outbreak on my chin and maybe I was a carrier. I asked the doctor if Jane could have contracted that from me. The doctor told us that it was possible, but not likely, since the strand of virus was of a different strand. Knowing that I wore protection with my deployment affairs, I turned to Jane and asked, "*Are you sure that you didn't catch something while you were in high school?*" Jane began to turn red in the face and remained silent to my question. The doctor reading the tension in the room said, "*I will prescribe you the medicine that you need. It will start to clear up after a week. It can remain dormant, but it can come back.*"

The car ride home was full of heated arguments. Jane started in with tears. "*Did you cheat on me?*"

"*No,*" I responded shifting in my seat and concentrating on the road ahead.

"*Well, I only kissed that guy I told you about months back, so I know that I didn't get it from him.*" "*I swear to you that I didn't cheat on you!*" she added.

"*Well, maybe you contracted it in high school and didn't know you were a carrier, and it finally showed up,*" I offered. Which didn't give me complete confidence because I knew I must have it too. Yet, I never contracted the virus. A week passed and Jane started to get really depressed. Since we had one vehicle, she dropped me off at the ship so she could use the car for errands and pick me up after work. She didn't show up to get me as usual that Monday. I called her cell, she didn't pick up. Getting frustrated, I began to walk home. Continuing to try and reach Jane on the phone, I became more and more upset after every attempt. I get home after walking 90 minutes.

I walk into the apartment and find Jane fast asleep in the bed. I nudge her awake and I ask her, "what happened to you today? "You were supposed to come and get me after work."

"*Oh, I must have fallen asleep,*" Jane replied.

Fuming from having to walk home, I demanded if she was going to stay home all day that I was going to take the car. Crying, she said, "*But I did go out and get groceries. I just got bored and went to sleep.*" I told her she needed to get a part-time job. She agreed and contested she would need the car to look for work tomorrow. The next day Jane forgot to pick me up again and I walked home attempting to reach her. She apologized. She continued to do this the rest of the week. Finally, I asked her, "*Are you okay?*"

She cried out, "*I'm depressed,*"

"*Why? Do you miss your family?*" I asked.

"*No, that's not it,*" Jane said sobbing.

"*Then what's the matter?*" I asked.

"*You're going to leave me if I tell you,*" She contested.

Then it dawned on me. This must be about the guy that she claimed she only kissed. I reassured her we could work it out if we talked about it. I wanted to get to rid of the guilt that I was carrying. So, if she was willing to confess, then I would too. I wanted honesty in our marriage.

"*I lied to you about...*" Jane said, through crying.

I waited patiently for her to tell me that she slept with another guy and that she was sorry, so that I can confess my infidelity too. She continues, "*I lied to you about being pregnant. I wanted to get out of a situation, and I used you. And I did sleep with that guy twice*".

Stunned, I didn't know what to say.

"*But, I do love you and I want to stay married to you,*" Jane, continued.

My head was spinning. I said, "*I need to go.*"

"*Where are you going,*" Jane asked.

"*I'm going to stay on the ship tonight.*"

Jane burst into tears, wailing and crying out, *"You're going to leave me aren't you?"* Jane cried.

"I gotta go, Jane, I need to think about this, I'll call you tomorrow." I managed.

I took our car and headed to the ship. "What just happened?" I thought. "Did she seriously just tell me that she used me?!" She said she lied about being pregnant. I remembered the conversation we had on the phone about what advice I would give to a friend who got a girl pregnant. She was feeling me out; she wondered if I would I take the bait or not? What else was a lie? Did she really love me? She finally told me the truth about the guy she slept with. Why would she tell me? Was she truly convicted, or did she figure that I would find out eventually? What was I to do? Could I trust her? Was there more that she was hiding? Or was she finally being transparent about the lies she was carrying because it was killing her to lie to someone who truly cared for her? If that was the case, what was my excuse? How easy would it be for me to go back to our apartment and confess that I went to strip clubs and slept with prostitutes? Something in me still did not want to divulge that information. I chose to be mad at Jane and hide my sin from her. I wanted her to suffer for the hurt she caused me. I wanted Jane to beg me to take her back. After three days of living on the ship and not communicating with her, I went home to our apartment. I found Jane in our closet crying with clothes torn from the hanger in piles on the floor. Crawling over to me sobbing she said, "*I'm so sorry Tim. I know I hurt you. Please don't leave me.*"

Silently staring at her, I remained motionless. My mind racing, flashing forward to what our future looked like together. Is this someone I wanted to constantly concern myself with if she was going to remain faithful to me? I asked Jane, "*What do you want from me, Jane?*" "*Wasn't I just a ticket out of your situation?*" "*You don't love me, you love YOU.*" "*The thought of you getting out of your hometown and getting to move to Hawaii was exciting to you. You wanted it so bad you didn't care who you lied to or who you hurt. It was all to benefit you. Now that you got what you strived and lied to get; you hate yourself for it. You don't want to lose it either, so here you are trying to right the wrong. Well, you can't erase all these lies with one apology, Jane. I thought I loved you, but I don't even know if I know you. I don't think this is going to work. Our marriage is built on lies.*"

Interrupting, Jane said, "*But we can start over, I have told you everything now, there are no more secrets. And I have come to fall in love with you. Please, Tim, give me another chance. I promise to win your heart every day. I'll be the wife of your dreams.*" Still on her knees, she began to undo my pants and I caved into my lust.

The next morning, Jane got up early and made breakfast. "*You're going to be late if you don't get up!*"

Jane announced. Continuing, she asked, *"Do you mind if I take you to work? I've got an interview for a job in the mall."*

"Sure, Jane, that's fine. Just be sure to pick me up Saturday morning, I'm on duty today and will be off at 9am on Saturday." I replied.

"Okie dokie!" Jane said. *"Hey,"* Jane continued, *"Do you mind if I come by your ship after working hours today, so I can tell you about my job interview?"*

"That's fine; just make sure it's after 4pm because that's when I'll get off of my watch." I said.

"Alrighty, 4:30pm it is!" Jane replied. Later that day, I was on my pier sentry watch and it was a quarter after 2pm. I had been walking up and down the pier guarding it with a 12 gauge shotgun strapped to my shoulder.

At about 300 yards up the pier, I noticed a short petite lady in civilian clothes walking up to the gate guard of the pier. After showing some identification, the gate guard let her in. She started walking hurriedly down the pier. As she got closer to me, I recognized that it was Jane. But what was she doing here so early? Didn't I tell her to come after 4 pm? It's just after 2pm; what in the world was she doing here? Fifty yards away I could see her facial expression, and she looked ticked off. At 10 yards, she started walking faster toward me because she recognized me in my uniform. With the same expression of anger, she started in, *"I can't believe you! I told you everything and you couldn't tell me that you went to strip clubs and slept with a prostitute! I hate you, you jerk!"*

Stunned, I replied. *"Excuse me!"* *"What are you talking about?"* Playing dumb to her accusations because I knew there were only two guys who knew what she was accusing me of and they were both on the ship. *"Ivan told me you and Matt were at strip clubs having a blast and bought prostitutes. How could you keep that from me, after I told you everything?"* Swinging to slap me, I caught her hand. *"HEY, YOU TWO!"* A shout came from my ship that was moored to the pier. We both turned to look. My hand still grasped around Jane's wrist. It was the Senior Chief Petty Officer and Duty section leader.

"YOU Two need to settle your affairs at home - preferably not around a loaded weapon. Ma'am, you need to go home. OS3 Avery, you need to get back on watch."

"Yes, Senior Chief!" I responded.

"Well, when you get home on Saturday I won't be there! I'm leaving! I'm flying home to my parents!" Jane said.

"Fine, Jane, do what you think is right."

"Oh, like you do what's right!? Screw you, Tim, we're done!" Jane fumed.

Later when I came off my shift, Senior Chief put his arm around my shoulder and said, *"Son, you need to be careful with the decisions that you make. Having an argument with a loaded weapon is not smart."*

I dreaded going home on Saturday. I knew Jane would be there. I knew we didn't have the money to get her a plane ticket home. Maybe her mom sprung for a ticket. I went to my friend's house and told him everything that happened. He was shocked. He asked, *"What are you going to do?"*

"I don't want the stress. We both messed up and I don't see how I can fix it. I lied. She lied. I think we should just get a divorce and move on. I'm tired of dealing with the stresses of it."

Later that evening, I went home to face Jane. I found Jane out on the balcony. The view from our 19th story apartment was spectacular, but I knew she wasn't out there enjoying the view. She was up on the railing looking down to the ground floor contemplating suicide is all I could gather. Wow, I thought, how did we get here? I went out there to ask if she was alright. Jane responded with *"get away from me, or I'll do it!"*

"Do what?" I asked, ignoring the obvious conclusion.

"I'll jump," Jane said, hesitantly. She continued *"Then you'll have to explain that to your command."*

"Jane, why don't we go inside and talk about this?" I asked.

"NO," Jane started. *"You lied to me even after I told you everything."*

"Jane, no one has to die. We both lied. Maybe we aren't meant to be together. That doesn't mean you need to kill yourself. You want to be happy, don't you?"

Tears streaming down her face, *"Yes, I do."* Jane replied.

"Then why don't we go inside and talk about it," I asked.

"Okay," Jane replied sobbing.

"Jane, I'm sorry that I lied to you. I should have told you. I held back the truth because I was mad at what you did. I didn't know what to do. I wanted you to hurt like you made me hurt. I'm so sorry."

After sitting for about an hour in silence, neither of us knowing what to say, Jane said, *"Well, I called my mom and she bought me a plane ticket. She said it would be a good idea that we separate for a while so that we each can think if this marriage is going to work or not."*

Taking a deep breath, I relented and said, *"Jane, that is probably the right thing to do. It will give us the break that we need and get the fresh start that we need to get to know each other."* She went to the bedroom and I slept on the couch.

The next day Jane flew home to her parents. We chatted on the phone at least once a week just to stay in touch. Keeping each other updated to what we were doing. Two weeks went by and my buddy Frankie invited me to go out to the club with him. I went with him. We made it a habit for the next three weeks. I started having fun again. The stress and worry started to disappear. I started to feel lonely. I loved having the companionship of a wife in my life, but I had to be able to trust her with my heart.

Chapter 9
Dawna Starr

It was a warm Friday night. I was stressed out and my buddy Frankie knew it. He suggested that we go out and have some fun at the clubs. Frankie wanted to check out Rumors night club. This was one of the largest nightclubs in Waikiki. It was in the ballroom of a swanky hotel. It had several dance floors, bars, and sitting areas. One of the cool features was that it had large columns throughout the place. When we arrived, the place was already packed with ladies. Free club entry and the first two drinks on the house for women was one sure way to pack a club. The line was out the door. As we made our way in the club, we knew it was going to be a good night. I was already buzzing from a bottle of rum we picked up along the way to the club. At that moment, a beautiful brown-eyed beauty came up to me and pulled me to the dance floor and said, *"You're coming with me!"* She had the most electrifying contagious smile. Within minutes, she left me on the dance floor. I was shocked! However, two other ladies started to dance with me, and I found myself looking for the one who had abandoned me! Looking over to the bar, I found her and mouthed, "*HELP ME!*" She replied back, "*You can take care of yourself. You know how to say, 'NO.' You're a grown man!*" then she walked away. "Wow! I thought. I had to meet that girl.

I shooed away the two nuisances because they were trying to take my shirt off. My curiosity was getting the best of me. I located the beautiful woman chatting with her friends at the bar. "*Can I buy you a drink?*" I asked.

"*Sure, what happened to your girlfriends?*" she asked sarcastically.

"*I think they were trying to get me kicked out by undressing me like that,*" I responded. She rolled her eyes with a playful smile and said, "*I'll have an apple martini*".

"*What's your name?*" I inquired. "*Dawna,*" she said.

"*I'm Tim. Hey, you want to dance?*" I asked.

"*No, not right now,*" Dawna said, chuckling, pointing to her drink.

"*Well, this is my friend Frankie,*" I said,

"*This is Amanda.*" Dawna said.

The four of us found a place to chat in the corner over a game of Pacman. We laughed about different things.

I said the corniest things and it made her belly laugh. She got my jokes. Then we got on the dance floor to dance. I was captured by Dawna's beauty.

Her big bright gorgeous smile, her soft, caramel skin, and her light brown eyes. After a couple of hours of dancing, we decided to get a bite to eat. The only place we knew that was opened that late was Denny's.

We headed there and had such a great time getting to know each other. Dawna was so intelligent, articulate, and goofy all at the same time. She truly encompassed the word beautiful. After the next couple of days, I wanted to see her again. She had been on my mind every moment of the day. I knew that I was still married to Jane, but I was starting to fall for Dawna. I didn't know what to do. Should I try and patch things up with Jane by starting over and choosing to forget how she used me to get married, and how I kept secrets from her?

It would take some time, but I was willing to make it work. Or should I call it quits with Jane and start anew with Dawna taking time to get to know her vowing to be open and honest with her? The night we met, we talked about our marital status. We were both in separation from our spouses. Conflicted, I was leaning towards getting back together with Jane, but I would have to forsake all others to do so. That meant if I really wanted to make it work, then I could not see Dawna again.

That Wednesday evening, Frankie and I had been hanging out at my apartment playing video games; my cell phone on the coffee table started to ring. I glanced over to see the name on the phone. It was Dawna. I had come to the conclusion that it was best that I ignore it. Knowing I was going to break her heart, she was better off not getting mixed up with me. I didn't want to hurt Dawna. Frankie noticed I was choosing to ignore my ringing phone, chimed in and said, *"Hey, man, are you going to get that?"*

"Nope." I responded.

"Why? Who is it?" Frankie asked. Taking a peek at the screen on my phone he saw Dawna's name and said, *"Hey, that's the girl from the club, isn't it? Why aren't you answering that? She was cute. And she is obviously into you."*

"Frankie, I'm still married, and I want to remain faithful to Jane."

"Well, there's nothing wrong with having a friend, Tim," Frankie contested. *"Just see what she wants,"* Frankie added.

Truth be told, I didn't want to hurt Dawna. Telling her my intentions would probably be best, so I grabbed my phone and answered it. *"Hello."* I answered.

"Hi, Tim, it's Dawna. Do you remember me?"

"Of course, I do. How could I forget that beautiful face?" I could see her smiling through the phone.

"Hey, I wanted to see what you were doing Friday and wanted to know if you wanted to go see a movie." Dawna asked.

"I don't know Dawna. I don't think that's a good idea. We're both married." Frankie jabbed his elbow in my rib and mouthed, *"You are just friends! Go!"*

"Dawna, all I can promise right now is that we go as friends."

"That's fine. I understand." Dawna continued, *"I wanted to see Radio. How about you?"*

"That's fine, what time did you want to go?"

"6 pm okay?" Dawna asked.

"Sure, that sounds good, can you come and get me? I sent my car to California." I asked.

"Sure, I'll come and get you about 5 pm." Dawna said.

"Okay, great! I'll see you then." I said.

"Okay. See you later, Tim!"

"Bye, Dawna."

"Bye, Tim".

"Uh oh, someone's got a hot date Friday night!" Frankie said teasing.

"Shut up Frankie!" I retorted.

Friday night came. Dawna was so beautiful. Her electric smile was dazzling. I couldn't help but smile. I told her I felt bad that she had to come across the island to get me, so that we could see a movie on her side of the island. I insisted that I pay for movie tickets and popcorn. She said, she didn't mind. Not knowing what to say, I asked her why she wanted to see *Radio*. She told me about how this movie was shot in her home state of South Carolina. The school that Radio, the main character, attended was T.L. Hanna, which Dawna's alma mater played for state titles in football.

We arrived at the theater and I purchased the tickets as promised. At the concession stand, Dawna asked for a big bucket of popcorn. That was fine until she rained salt on it and held it under a waterfall of melted butter. I chimed in and said. *"Hey, did you want any more popcorn with your salt and butter?"* She started belly laughing to the point of tears. Even I didn't think it was that funny but, she was so amused. We both enjoyed the movie. We started our drive back to my place. I felt it necessary to tell her the truth of my intentions of trying to make it work with Jane. I told her that I had a great time getting to know her, but I needed to try and make my marriage work. Dawna dropped me off at my place and we said our goodbyes.

Two weeks later I went to see Jane in California. I took a week of vacation from the military. Jane was her usual self, smoking and drinking, a typical party girl. I hated when she smoked. I asked her several times to quit. It was like kissing an ashtray every time she did. We went to one of Jane's girlfriends' house parties. We drank, but this time I noticed how flirtatious she was with a certain guy. I watched her as they chatted in the kitchen.

I walked into the kitchen to make my presence known. The guy, who was chatting with Jane, looked at me and walked away into another room. Slurring, Jane said, *"Hey, Babe, let's go into the bedroom."* Not amused, I stared at her blankly and told her that we needed to go. She asked me why, and I told her because she was drunk. She relented.

The next day she took me to her job. Jane started going to school when she arrived back in San Diego two months earlier.

She was studying to become a nursing assistant which I thought was good. She introduced me to the nurses she was working with, showing me off like a trophy husband. This catered to my ego, I must confess. The next day, Jane realized she was out of cigarettes. Good, I thought. It's a perfect time for her to quit. I told Jane, "*It's time you quit, Babe. It's not good for you. Let's get you some patches instead.*"

"*NO!*" She retorted. "*I need cigarettes!*" She demanded.

"*Well, I'm not spending any more money on them, so tough.*" I replied.

Breathing heavily now, she began to get upset.

I said, "*Are you serious right now? Are you really hyperventilating? Over cigarettes?*" I added.

"*Yes, you A-hole,*" Jane remarked. "*I'm having a panic attack!*"

"*Why?*" I asked. "*Because you can't have a cigarette?*"

"*Yes,*" she said, still breathing labored.

"*So, what happens if you don't get a cigarette?*" I asked sarcastically, not buying the whole panic attack bit.

"*I don't know, but I feel as if I'm going to pass out or die,*" she said.

Never having encountered someone having a panic attack, I didn't know what to do. I just kept on driving; hoping she would just calm down and the panic attack would subside. Or, she would give up the whole charade when she realized I wasn't going to cave in and buy her a pack of cigarettes. She started crying and pleading. Saying things like, "Don't you care for me?" Twenty minutes passed. She was still acting the same way. I begrudgingly, pulled over to a gas station and bought the cheapest pack of cigarettes they had. She thanked me, after pulling a lit cigarette up to her face and taking a drag.

Wow, I thought. Nicotine is seriously addicting? Is this what I had to look forward to? Later at her apartment, she told me. "*Hey, my friend wants us to head to the beach tonight; he has some weed for us. Can we go?*" Not wanting to have another outburst or panic attack for denying her another addicting drug, I agreed.

Part of me wanted to see her circle of friends. That would tell me all I needed to know if the relationship was something I wanted to pursue any further. Obviously, with drugs involved, that was going to be a big, NO. Would Jane be willing to let this lifestyle go for me? It didn't seem likely since she had a panic attack and would not relent from smoking cigarettes. I had to assume the best case scenario was a long shot.

We arrived at the beach around 9 p.m. She introduced me to her friends, Jack, Billy, and Krissy, -all of them already high. They asked us, "*Hey, you guys ready to get blazed up? We brought some 'shrooms' if you want to try, but it will cost you extra?*"

I told them I couldn't because I was in the military.

"*What about you, Jane? You ready?*" Jack asked.

"*Hell, yeah!*" she exclaimed.

The four of them climbed into Billy's truck, and I got back into my car and waited. Twenty minutes went by and Billy took his 4-wheel drive truck and drove closer to the water. They were about 200 yards away from me now. That's odd, I thought. My mind mulling over the possibilities of what they could be doing. I remembered Jack saying that they had 'shrooms,' but it would cost extra. Was she to pay for those drugs or was she just getting high with her friends? Did they move the truck to get another form of payment once they realized Jane didn't have any money? Boy, I hoped not. Why move the truck then? I knew she didn't have any cash. Thirty minutes went by and they came back and dropped Jane off to me, high as a kite.

"*You ready to go home?*" I asked.

Jane didn't respond. She just stared wide-eyed at her hand. Yup, this isn't the life I want to live, I concluded.

The next morning Jane slept in until about noon. I started thinking about Dawna. She didn't smoke or do drugs. Dawna told me she was miserable in her marriage. Maybe she was just about done with her marriage as I was with mine. I didn't see any reason to continue with my relationship to Jane.

When Jane finally stirred, I told her that we were done. *"I don't want to live this lifestyle, Jane."* I said.

"Whaat?" Jane mumbled, trying to focus.

"Jane, I don't believe that our marriage is going to work with you getting high, drinking, and sleeping around with other guys." I protested.

"Wait, how did you know, who told you that?" Jane asked.

"You just did. I'll file the paperwork when I get back to Hawaii and we'll go our separate ways." I called a cab to the airport and left her apartment.

I know that God continues to chase us down because He wants a relationship with us. He wants us to live a life holy and honoring to Him. I can relate to the story of the prodigal son. The father allowed his son to go and make his own choices. The son chose to live a dishonoring life. However, the life he chose was no longer producing freedom, but hardship. He was far away from the safety and abundance of his father's household. I believe if you are insistent on having your own way, the Father will allow you to choose what you think is best. Knowing that one day you will return to Him when your choice has proven false. I allowed lust to blind me from making clear decisions and choices. I fell in lust with Jane. I never truly loved her. Being blinded by my lust, I could not see nor heed the red flags and warning signs God was giving me. Marriage is a good thing and it needs to be made by two consenting adults who truly love each other, and most importantly, love the Lord.

When I got back to the ship the following day, my Chief pulled me aside and said "*OS3 Avery, the USS O'Kane can't conduct their one-week sea trial because they are short a rescue swimmer.*

Do you want to go help them out? If so, you'll need to leave tomorrow morning with them." Knowing that this was just the downtime I needed to process my personal life, I said, "*Sure, Chief.*"

"*Good then, I will let them know.*"

My chief told me that I wouldn't need to stand a watch, but to make myself available when they did their man overboard drills. Perfect, I thought. I called Dawna after work and told her I was back in town but would be out to sea for a week and wanted to know if she wanted to hang out when I got back into port. Dawna was excited to hear from me again. I'm sure that she had questions. I would fill her in with the details about Jane and me later. All I wanted to do was to take my time getting to know Dawna. I didn't want to rush into anything anymore and neither did she.

I had a lot of free time to think about my marriage to Jane. It is true what they say, "*That only fools rush into marriage.*" I had fallen into lust. I never took the time to really get to know Jane. We had a physical attraction towards each other; we both consumed alcohol and lied to each other. That was the foundation of our marriage. Sex, drinking, and lies were all it took for me to get hoodwinked into a marriage. The aftermath amounted to two wounded people with a tainted view on marriage.

Learn from my mistakes. If you are dating or seeing someone and your foundation is only sex, drinking, and lies, let me forewarn you; it will not turn out well. It will fall apart, and you will be worse off. As a father of an adult daughter, let me encourage you to make one of the two choices: (1) end the relationship or (2) both of you start a relationship with God. Notice, I didn't say go to church, although that's a start. I'm saying begin a relationship with God, Jesus, and the Holy Spirit. Let Them show you Who Love is and how to Be Love. Learn how They have loved you when you were at your worst.

Despite you not wanting anything to do with Them, They have still provided a way for you to live forever with Them in paradise.

Although you *feel* like They hadn't protected you from being harmed, They protected you from dying in your sin which would have made you eternally separated from God and heaven. Once you understand how to be loved, then and only then can you truly understand how to love another person, even when they have ugly flaws. Let's face it, we all have ugly flaws. Since God loves you in spite of your flaws, then we can learn to do the same.

Although it was easy duty, I was ready to get off the ship. While I was helping out the USS O'Kane with their sea trials, the Navy released the results of the E-5 exam, and I got promoted to E-5. I was so excited! When I stepped off the boat, Dawna was standing there waiting. She was a sight for sore eyes. What a knockout!

I told her everything about what happened with Jane. She told me that her relationship with her husband was over, too. We filed our divorces in the same month. The weekend I got back into port with the USS O'Kane, I asked Dawna what her plans were for the weekend. She said, "*Hanging out Saturday with my friends and our kids.*" Dawna had told me she had a daughter named

Sophia from a previous marriage. I said, "*Well, I have duty Saturday. What are you doing Sunday?*"

"*I'm going to church,*" Dawna said.

Church, now there's a place that I hadn't been since I was a teenager. I loved the people there and felt the love there. I knew that it was something that I was missing in my life. I had given my life to Christ when I was 13. I felt different like something changed in me. I felt love without an agenda for the first time. However, a few months later, I stopped going. Nobody else in my family went. I was practically sneaking out on Wednesday nights just to go to church.

I asked Dawna if I could go with her. She said, "*Sure, you can go.*" I thought she would be impressed that I wanted to go with her. Later, I found out that she had heard this line from guys before who said they wanted to go to church with her, only not to show up.

Sunday morning came, and she picked me up on base. I met Sophia, short and pretty, little, blonde-haired, and blue-eyed girl. Not what I was expecting. This was a stark contrast from Dawna's caramel skin, dark hair, and brown eyes. This girl was your typical Caucasian kid and Dawna, for all intents and purposes, your typical Latin beauty. I thought to myself, Sophia's dad has some serious dominant genes. Her daughter looked nothing like her, at first glance. As I took notice of their facial features, they both had the same eye shape and smile lines. Sophia's response to me was just as shocking. She blurted out to her mom. "*WHO is THAT?*"

I didn't know if she was being protective at 9 years old and didn't approve or thought I was handsome. I figured the latter. Later, I find out that she was being protective.

I also met her roommate's kids, Keanna and Braven. What an awesome family! As we got to the church, I was getting nervous. Here I am walking into a church with another man's wife and they all knew. I didn't feel any judgment though. Dawna introduced me to her longtime big brothers in Christ, Brad and Napoleon. These brothers were like bodyguards. I sensed they really looked out for the people there, especially Dawna and Sophia. Both were married and their wives greeted Dawna warmly. As we took our seats, I could feel the presence of love there. I could sense concern from the ladies that Dawna embraced. Some even whispered in her ear. Dawna reassured them with her words. They smiled and introduced themselves to me. I understood the concern they had for Dawna. From what I learned, her previous husband was abusive and never went to church with her. Here I was a stranger, coming to church with her.

The service started and the praise and worship was emotionally moving. I could feel people genuinely worshipping God. I felt a stirring in me. I had flashes of memories that happened to me in that past year. After a while, the pastor came out and started preaching. I didn't know what the sermon was about. I just knew if this man gave an altar call, I was going up there to give my life back to Christ. I was going through so much on my own, and I needed Him back in my life. I was tired of trying to figure out what to do. I was tired of not being able to trust. So, I went up to the front and rededicated my life to God.

From that moment on, Dawna and I saw each other regularly. Our divorces were finalized in the same month. We dated for a full year. My walk with God strengthened but there were a lot of things that needed to be rooted out. I had a huge lust problem. I still looked at other women. I didn't think it was a problem. Dawna had confronted me with the looking many times. I felt like a hypocrite anyway; here I was living with a woman that I wasn't married to, but she wanted me to stop looking at other women because it was considered lust. So, I modified my behavior around Dawna.

Going to church Sunday after Sunday really started to take effect on me. I was getting convicted of something different every time. I remember leaving a church service one Sunday and after being so moved and convicted by the service, I stopped wanting to listen to secular music. God was changing things in my life. I had given Him the reigns of my soul and now HE was working on my mind, will, and emotions. The Holy Spirit was rooting out the bad music laced with horrible lyrics that promoted a promiscuous lifestyle. There were many other things the Lord began to deal with me on, including the friends that I was around. I stopped hanging around them. I met other Christians. I stopped going to clubs and chasing women. I wanted to marry Dawna but there was something she insisted that I do. Especially since this was to be my second and her third marriage.

Chapter 10
Working out my Healing

Confrontation

Before getting married, Dawna insisted that I confront my Dad. It was not an easy thing to do, but I knew it was a part of my healing journey.

We flew to my hometown in California, and I introduced my fiancé to my mom and my sisters. My dad and mom had soon separated after I left for the Navy. My sister finally told my mom what was happening, and it needed to stop. After having an open family conversation about what happened when we were younger, tears and apologies came forth to bring reconciliation. It strengthened our relationship. It renewed family unity and trust. A great deal of healing took place in that living room. All condemnation, shame, worry, and guilt left the people in that living room. The only person who wasn't present was my father. I asked my older sister if she'd ever confronted dad about what he did to us. She said, yes, and that all he did was deny it. I was enraged. I asked where he lived. Dawna and I drove over to his apartment. When we got out of the car, my knees were weak. I noticed a small boy playing outside of my dad's apartment door. I knocked on the door with my heart pounding. Thinking and rehearsing what I might say, I knew it wasn't going to be easy. Rage started to rise in me from thinking about all the things my father had put me through.

I knocked again with more force this time. Nobody answered the door. As we looked through the half-covered windows of my father's apartment, Dawna said she could feel a demonic presence. It was really eerie. Plus, the five-year-old, biracial boy playing innocently in the front grassy area of my dad's apartment made me sick to my stomach. I knew that if I didn't confront my dad and alert this neighborhood of the pedophile living among them, this boy could be a potential target. What I saw in this boy was me. I wished that someone would have protected me from such pain and horror.

We went back to my car and waited until my dad got home. All I could fixate on was the small boy playing outside. Dawna knew what I was thinking and said, *"You can save that boy from being molested by your dad, just like you wished someone would have saved you."* At that moment, Dawna insisted that we pray in tongues and allow the Holy Spirit to invigorate us with the strength and guidance of what to say. After a time of prayer, we waited a little longer, and finally, I spotted my dad's car whipping into a parking space. He got out and glanced down at the boy playing near his front door. I immediately got out; Dawna right at my heels. I called out to my dad; he turned around with a light-hearted, *"Hey, Son, how are you?"*

I responded with *"Not good, dad, not good at all."*

He had a perplexed look on his face and responded with *"What's up son?"*

My throat thickened and all I could get out was, *"You know what you did?"*

The sign of understanding hit his face, but he responded with *"What do you mean?"*

I repeated my accusation. *"You know what you did to me!"*

His response was,. *"I don't know what you're talking about."* He turned and continued to his door.

I pursued with, *"You molested me."*

With a quick retort he sounded *"No, I didn't."*

At that moment, Dawna sprang in front of me and got right between my father and me. My dad and I are both well over six feet tall, but that didn't stop Dawna's five-foot two stature from getting in my dad's face. My dad quickly threw up his hands in defense and backed off. Dawna leaned closer. Dawna in a stern, soft voice, commanded him to stop lying. We knew what happened and he owed his son an apology. My dad asked Dawna, *"Are you his therapist? Then you help him."*

Dawna countered with a strong and demanding tone, *"He is your son and he has some questions, and you WILL answer him!"*

His eyes now fixed on mine. I asked the most logical question I could ask. *"Why did you do those things to me?"*

His response rang loudly in my ears and penetrated deep into my heart and soul. *"I thought you liked it."*

I became enraged and spouted off, *"You thought I liked you doing those things to me?! I was young; I was intimidated; I was your son; why couldn't you just love me?"* Tears of pain welled up in me.

After a moment of silence, my dad responded with "*Is that all you remember? Did I not take you fishing and to see wrestling?*"

"*Dad, you hurt me and my sisters, and you continue to deny what you did.*"

"*What are you going to do, kill me?*" He interjected.

"*No, I forgave you and I'm going to let God deal with you, but you will never see your grandkids until you repent.*"

Dawna and I walked back to the car and left. I felt a sigh of relief. I had confronted my abuser, my father. But, what was I supposed to do with the "*I thought you liked it*" remark? Deep down I knew that the sensation of being touched was pleasurable.

I felt guilty because the sensation did feel good. Did I like it? Is that why my dad persisted? I got an answer from the question I longed to ask, but did that answer help me heal? Or did it make me worse off? Now what? Was I to bury those thoughts and emotions? Although I confronted my abuser, I felt worse off than I did before I confronted him. What I got was an answer that led me to believe that it was my fault. He thought I liked it. The truth is I couldn't recall a time I resisted. Great, I thought, what was I supposed to do with this new information?

Dawna looked over at me. *"Honey, are you okay? I'm really proud of you."*

All I could say was how impressed I was of her, standing up to my dad like that. Wow, what a fierce woman I have! She beamed with the smile, but then quickly asked again noticing the troubled look on my face. *"Are you okay?"*

"He thought I liked it." I said. Dawna looked at me with compassion, *"I know, Honey, and I'm sorry."*

In the few months of dating, Dawna and I moved in together. We slept together and were still going to church. In fact, even though I gave my life to Christ, I still struggled with my lust addictions. I thought for sure that by giving my life over to Him the lust would go away on its own. I asked God to take the lust and the desire to look at other women. God did not heal me instantly from it.

But, He answered my prayer...

And do not be conformed to this world, but be transformed by the renewing of your mind, that you may prove what is that good and acceptable and perfect will of God. Romans 12:2

Six months prior to our wedding day, God sent me on deployment with my new command in San Diego.

Mainly because God told us to remain pure before our wedding day, and we were not being obedient to Him.

I befriended a Christian brother named Marshall while I was on deployment. Marshall was the friend I needed to help me stay focused on the Lord. I was a baby Christian and I needed the accountability to help keep my heart focused on Christ. I thank God for Marshall. He had struggled with pornography in his past as well. But he was a lot further along in his journey than I was. He and I studied the Bible together. When I needed a confidant on some struggles, he was there to offer support, encouragement, and prayers.

Before we left on deployment, I picked up a copy of *CLEAN*, by Dr. Doug Weiss, a porn and sexual addiction recovery workbook. This was a tough process. I had to get honest with myself. I had to write down the things that happened to me. I had to journal what I was thinking. It really helped me to identify the truth about sex and why it was created.

It helped me realize that the events in my life contributed to the way sex was distorted and perverted to me. It showed me how to pray. It helped me to be equipped with prayers to keep my mind focused on Christ. I wanted to be open and honest with Dawna to the point where I showed her every journal entry and thought I had. That was a mistake. Don't do that. All she really wanted to know was that I was getting help for the addiction. I wore a rubber band around my wrist and snapped it every time I had an impure thought. I related the pain I felt to the pain that I was causing Dawna with every thought. I trashed all of the R-rated movies that I had in my possession on the ship. I also got rid of any movies I knew had sex scenes in them. I learned those were triggers in releasing an onslaught of stored images on the mental hard drive of my brain. I changed the music I listened to. I went all out in trashing all music that promoted sexual promiscuity or the degrading of women. I started a collection of Christian artists with various genres.

It was the beginning of my journey. Now that I was a new creature in Christ Jesus, my mind was being transformed. Romans 12:2. 1 Peter 1:13.

My new developing character was tested on the deployment by a Chief Warrant Officer. He was sending and sharing pornographic pictures to guys he thought were cool enough to not say anything. When he showed me a picture that he had saved on his phone, he asked, *"So, what do you think OS2? Hot, right?"*

"Whoa, ah Sir, I would appreciate that you wouldn't show me stuff like that. I'm a Christian and I'm married." I replied. I noticed the wedding band on his finger.

"Ah, no problem OS2! I'll make sure not to do that." Startled by my response and realizing he crossed a line with a subordinate that probably could have gotten him demoted or even kicked out of the military, had I reported him.

He was the nicest person to me on the deployment. He even offered to cover a watch for me while we were pulled into port so that I could have an extra day of liberty to see the sites in Singapore.

I told Marshall about it and he was shocked. I asked him if I should turn him in. He told me, *"I wouldn't if he stopped."*

"God gave him a good enough scare to get him to straighten up. "You did your part by resisting the temptation, Tim. I'm proud of you and you know God is proud of you"

The enemy will keep on testing you like he did Jesus. But every time the enemy tried to test Jesus, Jesus always hit Satan with a truth scripture. In that, Jesus gave us the play-by-play of how to get the enemy to flee. Matt 4:1-11, Luke 4:1-13.

In the fall of 2004, I got home from what I called a successful deployment. I was able to start my healing journey. Dawna had planned two weddings for us: One in Hawaii for her longtime friends and the other in San Diego for our families in California.

 The first wedding was scheduled the day we pulled in to Hawaii, our last stop on the deployment, before the ship went to its homeport of San Diego.

Dawna was so beautiful in the traditional Hawaiian wedding dress. She was wearing several flower leis adorned by her friends. She wore a beautiful crown on her head made out of beautiful Hawaiian flowers. She bought me a Hawaiian dress shirt to match. I had leis placed on me from friends. The weather, as always, was amazing in Hawaii. It was a beautiful ceremony held at the aptly named Magic Island. Dawna arranged the perfect day. I was truly overjoyed by the Lord's grace and goodness.

To cap off the evening at the reception, we slow danced to "Overjoyed" by Stevie Wonder. God was doing something beautiful by His grace. We were at the beginning of our road of marriage.

The three of us made our move to San Diego. Since my ship was offering a family cruise from Hawaii to San

Diego, Sophia got moved to San Diego in style on an aircraft carrier. Dawna couldn't join us because she was a spouse, only kids of sailors or marines were allowed to ride. Some said they made that rule because no one would get any work done with spouses onboard.

We got settled into a place in San Diego. After a year of being stationed on the Aircraft carrier, I got orders to be an instructor at the Rescue Swimmer School in San Diego. I was excited because that meant I wasn't attached to a ship for three years; I didn't have to deploy, and I had reached my shore duty status.

We took time nurturing our marriage - learning from the mistakes from our previous marriages. We attended a marriage enrichment weekend that the Navy paid for. We really learned a lot about each other and how each thought and the past hurts that we went through. That weekend really strengthened our marriage. We vowed to do something like that every year to invest in our marriage. We got rooted in a church and started attending regularly. That following year, we bought a condo in the outskirts of San Diego, and started attending an extended campus of Shadow Mountain Church where we not only attended but served.

As I was getting settled in at my new command, I got word from my chief that I was selected for Individual

Augmentee (IA) orders to deploy with Seal Teams 1 and 2.

"What?" I thought. *"How is that even possible?"* I questioned my Chief.

"Needs of the military, OS2. They can select and move anybody around they want to fight in a war effort." My Chief said and followed up with *"Looks like you're billeted to leave in two months for training at Fort Jackson, SC for two weeks followed up with a nine-month deployment to Iraq."*

I told Dawna and Sophia about the news. We all cried, but then we asked God to take care of us of all while we were apart. After I got back from deployment, Dawna and I made a pact that we were done with the military life. I count it an honor to have served my country, but for Dawna and me, the time came for us to find something different that would enrich our marriage. After three years of making San Diego our home and building a business opportunity that could help us transition out, I finished my commitment to the Navy. God placed it on our hearts to move to Dawna's hometown of Gaffney, SC.

A year later after getting settled into South Carolina, I got a phone call from my older sister. She told me that my dad's sister, Aunt Margaret, called to say that dad had breast cancer. It had gotten into his blood and they put him in hospice and he might not make it another week. I told her to thank Aunt Margaret.

As much as I hated what my dad did to me, I didn't want him to go to hell. I wanted him to be forgiven by God just as I was. I'd forgiven my dad for what he did. I knew he had been a deacon of a church during the first few years we lived in California. Since then, he had fallen away from the faith. I wanted to make sure with absolute certainty that he was saved.

I called up my pastor who knew a little bit about my testimony. I told him my dad was on his deathbed and I wanted to make sure he was saved. Do you mind calling him with me?

He agreed. I dialed the number given to me that would reach my father's bedside. My pastor was on three-way. My aunt answered the phone. *"Hello?"* she asked.

"Hi, this is Tim Avery,"

My aunt said in a loving voice, *"It's good to hear from you. I'll put your dad on."*

I could hear my Aunt tell my dad it was your son calling. After hearing some other voices in the background, I could tell that my dad's siblings and family were there at his bedside.

"Hello, Son," he weakly muttered.

"Hi, Dad. How are you doing?"

"I'm doing okay, Son." He said.

"Dad, I'm calling you to tell you that I'm sorry for the way I confronted you. I was angry and frustrated. Will you forgive me?"

"NO, I won't," he responded.

What seemed like an eternity of silence after that harsh response, I spoke and said, *"Dad, I know that I hurt you with how I confronted you, will you forgive me? I have forgiven you. I'm calling to make sure that you have a relationship with God."*

His response still seemed strange; He said he was a traveler and when he was done with this life, he would come back in another form. I never heard my dad speak of anything like this before. I knew my pastor was quietly listening and waiting for me to bring him in though it was strange. My dad kept going on this "traveler" rant until his voice became faint.

Then one of my uncles grabbed the phone and said, *"Timmy, this is your Uncle Charles, your dad is on a lot of medication right now. It seems that he is asleep right now. He's very weak. You can try calling again tomorrow if you'd like."*

"Thanks, Uncle Charles, I appreciate that." I responded.

"*Goodbye, Son.*" Uncle Charles said.

After he hung up, I had a long conversation with my pastor. I asked, "*What did you think about what he said about being a traveler?*"

"*Well, it sounds like he got into some Far East religion. That's my guess since he kept talking about coming back.*"

After I got off the phone, I prayed that God would give me peace, a peace that I tried to win my dad to Christ, and that I would be free from the guilt of hating my father of what he did to our family. A couple of days later, my Aunt Margaret called to tell me my dad had passed and that she was sorry for having to tell me. She proceeded to tell me when and where the funeral would be. I blanked out on her relaying the details of the funeral. I had flashes of good memories of my father taking me fishing.

Then I thanked her for telling me and hung up the phone. Then peace came. I didn't cry. I just had peace. I went to church the next Sunday to tell my pastor and he embraced me and said, "*It's up to the Lord now, Tim.*"

He asked how I was doing. I told him I was still processing, yet I had an overwhelming peace and calmness about me. I didn't go to my father's funeral. It would have been too hard for me to be there. I still don't know for sure if my father made it to heaven. I don't carry the guilt if he did or didn't. I had the closure I needed. I got to ask for forgiveness and receive forgiveness from my father.

There will be trials; there will be failures. These are meant to refine the gold that is in you. Every trial and every failure should cause you to learn and to grow from them. They are never meant to stop, prevent, deny, delay, or block you from finishing the race that's before you. Although it has stopped you before, you will always have the choice to begin again, to continue, to learn how to overcome the obstacle, so that you can win the trial. To rise above adversity. To overpower the enemy's lies with the truth and power of God's word and the blood of Jesus Christ. The truth is that you are a son/daughter of God adopted through the finished work of Christ Jesus.

Galatians 4:4-7 - This makes you MORE than a conqueror.

Romans 8:37 - You have a rightful place to rule as a joint heir in Christ's Kingdom.

What's the end goal of your life? In Genesis 15:1, God tells Abraham whom he gave all the promises to that we get to live out, "*I am your exceedingly great reward.*" As we endure this race, we call life; we need to understand God is our reward. I'm not talking about the limited relationship that we are currently now having with Him because of our finite bodies.

I'm talking about having the relationship that our loved ones who have gone before us and are at His throne, getting to see Him face to face; experiencing His very love flowing through them as a tangible force. Seeing the heaven that He created with all beauty and majesty that makes the most beautiful places on earth look like a dump in comparison. To be able to live in heaven where sin no longer exists because it will be cast into the lake of fire. An eternity of free food, peace, and no taxes. And everyone said, "AMEN!"

What then is the purpose of your life? Colossians 1:16 says, "*All things were created through him and for him.*"

We were made to bring honor and glory to Jesus the preeminent one. What does that mean? That means the gifts and talents that were given to you were on purpose. The desires of wanting to be a doctor, architect, lawyer, electrician, pilot, nurse, pastor, evangelist, truck driver, teacher, actor, singer, stay-at-home mom or dad, God put that desire in you when He created you in your mother's womb. As you get older, those desires start to come out. The great news is that everything that we do should bring honor and glory to God. After all, He created you just for Him.

Colossians 3:23 tells us that "*And whatever you do, do it heartily, as to the Lord and not to men. Knowing that from the Lord you will receive the reward of the inheritance; for you serve the Lord Christ.*" The purpose of your career is Christ.

Chapter 11
Satan's Role

"Be sober; be vigilant; because your adversary the devil walks about like a roaring lion, seeking whom he may devour. Resist him, steadfast in the faith, knowing that the same sufferings are experienced by your brotherhood in the world." 1 Peter 5:8

I want to give you something to think about. Up to this point, you have been reading my story. Hopefully, you have seen the error of my ways and are doing what's necessary to change the trajectory for your life. There is one more thing that I wanted to tackle in this book. This next section of my book is about exposing the enemy.

As I told you and what you've probably already heard is that Satan wants to remain unseen. This is the best tactic for any opponent... you can't see them, or you don't even know they are there, or even worse, you don't think they exist. As I write this, I am reminded of the movie, "Pearl Harbor." Based on the Pearl Harbor attack, which was considered successful because Japan was able to keep their plans a secret up until the very moment of their well thought out and then well-executed attack. They were able to fly under the radar long enough to be undetected. When the Americans started to become suspicious of Japan's strange naval fleet movements in the Pacific, Japan reassured the Americans with peace medals and peace agreements. They didn't want to be seen as an enemy. To the Americans, Japan didn't exist as an enemy.

Friends, Satan hates you and he wants nothing more than to destroy you, but even more than that, he wants to use God, your Creator, to destroy you and remain undetected as your enemy.

Let's talk about Satan for a moment. He was known as Lucifer, son of the morning. Why was he created? What was his function? In Ezekiel 28:11-19, we are told who Lucifer is and why he was created and then his demise.

He was created to protect the very throne of God. He was able to see the very power of God up close and personal. He saw how every created being worshipped God with complete honor and respect. And he placed his seal of perfection on it if the worship was genuine.

Although he was created perfect and beautiful and full of wisdom, he wanted more. He wanted the very throne of God. He wanted to be worshipped like God was worshipped. He didn't want to serve God anymore. He wanted to be like GOD.

I believe, although Lucifer lost his role in heaven, he still does what he was created to do, except now it is with a different agenda. Instead of testing the love of God in all creation and placing the seal of perfection on it, he accuses all created beings not following God's commandments. Even to the point of setting traps or temptations for the human race to fall into sin so they are punished according to God's law. Because Satan is created with the wisdom of the heavenly courts, it makes him an effective tempter and lawyer. Clearly stated, Satan is a legalist. In heaven, there is a courtroom where God is the Judge, Jesus is the defender, the hosts of heaven are the witnesses and Satan is the accuser of all men ensuring that all men are upholding God's law. *"If they aren't obeying the Law of God then they need to be punished like me. You are a just God and Your word shall not return to You void."* Satan says assuredly.

"Who and what accusations are you bringing up to the courts of heaven today, Satan?" Jesus asks, almost smiling.

"Jehovah God Almighty, just in all His ways, may I present to You, Timothy James Avery for Your review. These are true and accurate accusations, my Lord. He is a lustful and prideful man. He has broken every one of Your commandments. He has made sex his god, He has taken Your name in vain. He has not observed a Sabbath day. He hates his father. He has repeatedly committed adultery. He has stolen from his best friend. He has slept with a married woman. According to Your law, oh King of Kings, he is to die." Satan demands.

"Father, Satan's accusations are true and correct."

"See, even Your son admits it, he is to die" Satan interjects.

"Father," Jesus continues. *"Timothy James Avery has given his life to me and he has made me Lord and Savior of his life, so all of these sins and future sins are paid for by the blood that I shed."* Timothy James Avery is your son, oh King!" Jesus proclaimed.

"Gabriel, throw this case file out. Timothy James Avery's name is written in the Lambs book of life. Michael, throw Lucifer out of my courtroom!" God declares.

"Yes, Your majesty, with pleasure!" Both Archangels declare in unison. Rev 20:12, Luke 10:20, psalms 69:28.

"I'll be back, Jesus, they all haven't given themselves over to you, you wait and see you're going to have to banish

more of them to Hell with me!" Satan declared. 1 Peter
1:3-5

Chapter 12
How God Turned My Mess into a Message

"And we know that all things work together for good to those who love God, to those who are the called according to His purpose. For whom He foreknew, He also predestined to be conformed to the image of His Son, that He might be the firstborn among many brethren. Moreover whom He predestined, these He also called; whom He called, these He also justified; and whom He justified, and these He also glorified." - Romans 8:28-30

Up to this point, you have been reading my story and you have seen how the enemy can take a person's life and do his best to ruin it with his tactics and temptations. Now, I want to show you how God has turned it all around, thus making beauty out of my ashes.

When I arrived in South Carolina in January 2009, our daughter had been there the previous fall to start high school. She had been attending a church called Restoration Church Gaffney. The worship and message there were incredible. Dawna and I got involved in the youth and in the production. We even started a fitness class there called *Fit for the Kingdom*. Our passion for God grew so much we started having the youth come over to our house and held worship sessions and studied the word.

After sharing my testimony with them, they wanted to share the goodness of God in their lives. They brought friends, teens, and young adults. They were getting saved in our home. It was so amazing to see the power of God come on those young people in our home.

Dawna and I were asked to be a part of a big play production at our church titled, "*The Power of the Blood.*" Dawna and Sophia were asked to dance in the production, and I got the high honor of playing

Jesus. The experience of playing our Savior caused me to fall deeper in love with Him. I got to see through His eyes how He loves you and me so much. What a passionate Savior we serve!

I was so moved, that in the marketplace at my job, I began to witness to my coworkers. I invited them all to see the production. Most of them came and brought their families and friends. I started to apply God's principle of doing my work as unto Him and not man. After several weeks of doing this, I was promoted at my job and was offered a program that would have put me into a management track. At the same time, God was growing our direct sales business focused on nutrition. I was two weeks away from putting in my two-week notice. God was blessing Dawna and me.

We moved to Spartanburg to grow our business. We got involved at Evangel Cathedral and started helping with the youth teaching courses on purity and the truth of the influence of music. We led breakout sessions for youth conferences. Dawna was asked to come on staff at Evangel Cathedral to be the Assistant Administrator and Director of Connections to the Lead Pastor, Dr. Langley. I coached the church's boys' basketball team. The boys and I had so much fun. We never won a game but, those guys loved every minute of it; so did I. Thinking back on it now makes me smile. Most of the teenagers and young adults that God brought into our lives to mentor are all currently doing ministry or impacting the marketplace with the love and witness of Christ.

As Evangel Cathedral transitioned to becoming Free Chapel Spartanburg, an extended campus of Jentezen Franklin Ministries, Dawna continued on staff with a new role as Administrative Assistant and Accounting.

God was showing favor and elevating us. Later, I was offered to come on staff as the Connections Pastor and Facilities Supervisor. I happily accepted. Dawna and I were on staff together at a growing and thriving church. We taught discipleship courses, facilitated assimilation, led the volunteer's team, implemented a leadership track for key volunteers and enjoyed assisting in the launch of Young Adults at our campus. God was using us, His children, to encourage and stir up the leadership gifts in those that served at this campus.

When God called us to resign from Free Chapel to launch Visual Testaments, we knew it would be difficult because we loved what we were doing and the people so much! We needed to be sure that it was

Him calling us to resign. For months we were in prayer and seeking after Him.

Finally, after two weeks of solid confirmations, we were reassured with His answer in very specific ways. We knew that being in His will is the best will to be in! Since then, we have shared our messages of hope in three different states. We have partnered with two other ministries to show and testify the glory of God. We have been on TV interviews, and now officially authors, since God had put it on our hearts to write our books testifying of His goodness in our lives. He is so amazing! If you trust Him with your life, who knows where He will take you!

Conclusion: Your story matters too!

Most, if not all, stories are written in a way where good ultimately triumphs over evil. As humans, we love when justice prevails, that is why we love stories like these. Think of all your favorite movies that have either made you laugh, cry, or excited that good triumphed over evil. Most stories start with the main character having either a bad start leading to a great victory; or the character has a great start and then experiences a tragedy mid-story and then the tragedy was overcome in some way. We love stories of hope! It breathes a renewed life onto our own stories.

The point is that stories or "testimonies" bring hope for personal healing. We think, if that person can experience a reconciled life after their tragedy, then so can I. This is why it is important for all of us to share our stories. They are all powerful, yet not everyone will be able to connect to my story. This is where you come in. Your full story may not have the redemptive ending yet. Well, honestly if you think about it, none of our stories do on this side of heaven. Yet, there are chapters of your life that you can share where God did something to heal, restore, or redeem you. Your story, no matter how insignificant you think it is, will bring hope to another person.

Revelation 12:11 says *"And they overcame him by the blood of the lamb and by the word of their testimony and they did not love their lives to the death."*

What will you share with another person today that can bring them hope?

Tim leading the volunteer teams at Free Chapel

Tim and Dawna baptized in the Jordan River by Pastor Jentezen Franklin, Tim got to help baptize with Pastor Jentezen on this trip in 2016

BIG FAM PIC
(Avery Family with
Rutland Family, 2016)

Tim ministering at Worship Outdoors, led by Larry and Jackie Christopherson in Spartanburg, SC

Tim and Dawna on
NITE LINE TV promoting
Visual Testaments Ministry

Tim being by ordained with CLST Global by Dr. Randal S. Langley

Tim and Dawna preaching at Life Chapel in Rainsville, Alabama 2018

Tim and Dawna praying during a service at Free Chapel Spartanburg Campus

Arsenal of Scriptures That Helped Me

I Corinthians 6:15-20

Do you not know that your bodies are members of Christ? Shall I then take the members of Christ and make them members of a harlot? Certainly not! Or do you not know that he who is joined to a harlot is one body with her? For "the two," He says, "shall become one flesh." But he who is joined to the Lord is one spirit with Him. Flee sexual immorality. Every sin that a man does is outside the body, but he who commits sexual immorality sins against his own body. Or do you not know that your body is the temple of the Holy Spirit who is in you, whom you have from God, and you are not your own? For you were bought at a price; therefore glorify God in your body and in your spirit, which are God's.

Romans 6:5-7

For if we have been united together in the likeness of His death, certainly we also shall be in the likeness of His resurrection, knowing this, that our old man was crucified with Him, that the body of sin might be done away with, that we should no longer be slaves of sin. For he who has died has been freed from sin

Romans 6:11-13

Likewise you also, reckon yourselves to be dead indeed to sin, but alive to God in Christ Jesus our Lord. Therefore do not let sin reign in your mortal body, that you should obey it in its lusts. And do not present your members as instruments of unrighteousness to sin, but present yourselves to God as being alive from the dead, and your members as instruments of righteousness to God.

Romans 6:14-16

For sin shall not have dominion over you, for you are not under law but under grace. What then? Shall we sin because we are not under law but under grace? Certainly not! Do you not know that to whom you present yourselves slaves to obey, you are that one's slaves whom you obey, whether of sin leading to death, or of obedience leading to righteousness?

Romans 8:1-2

There is therefore now no condemnation to those who are in Christ Jesus, who do not walk according to the flesh, but according to the Spirit. For the law of the Spirit of life in Christ Jesus has made me free from the law of sin and death.

Romans 8:13-14

For if you live according to the flesh you will die; but if by the Spirit you put to death the deeds of the body, you will live. For as many as are led by the Spirit of God, these are sons of God

Romans 8:33-35

Who shall bring a charge against God's elect? It is God who justifies. Who is he who condemns? It is Christ who died, and furthermore is also risen, who is even at the right hand of God, who also makes intercession for us. Who shall separate us from the love of Christ? Shall tribulation, or distress, or persecution, or famine, or nakedness, or peril, or sword?

I Peter 1:3-4

Blessed be the God and Father of our Lord Jesus Christ, who
according to His abundant mercy has begotten us again to a living hope through the resurrection of Jesus Christ from the dead, to an inheritance incorruptible and undefiled and that does not fade away, reserved in heaven for you,

I Peter 5:8-11

Be sober; be vigilant; because your adversary the devil walks about like a roaring lion, seeking whom he may devour. 9 Resist him, steadfast in the faith, knowing that the same sufferings are experienced by your brotherhood in the world. 10 But may the God of all grace, who called us to His eternal glory by Christ Jesus, after you have suffered a while, perfect, establish, strengthen, and settle you. To Him be the glory and the dominion forever and ever. Amen.

Philippians 4:8-9

Finally, brethren, whatever things are true, whatever things are noble, whatever things are just, whatever things are pure, whatever things are lovely, whatever things are of good report, if there is any virtue and if there is anything praiseworthy—meditate on these things. 9The things which you learned and received and heard and saw in me, these do, and the God of peace will be with you.

Ephesians 6:11

Put on the whole armor of God that you may be able to stand against the wiles of the devil. For we do not wrestle against flesh and blood, but against principalities, against powers, against the rulers of the darkness of this age, against spiritual hosts of wickedness in the heavenly places.

2 Corinthians 5:17

Therefore, if anyone is in Christ, he is a new creation; old things have passed away; behold, all things have become new.

Romans 8:28-30

"And we know that all things work together for good to those who love God, to those who are the called according to His purpose. For whom He foreknew, He also predestined to be conformed to the image of His Son, that He might be the firstborn among many brethren. Moreover whom He predestined, these He also called; whom He called, these He also justified; and whom He justified, these He also glorified."

Additional Resources

Clean: A Proven Plan for Men Committed to Sexual Integrity
Dr. Douglas Weiss
www.drdougweiss.com

XXX Church: Helping people break from porn addiction
X3 watch online accountability
Craig Gross
www.xxxchurch.com

Prayers "Little Red Prayer Book,"
Richard Broadbent III
App available
www.christianword.org

Report sexual abuse
www.Rainn.org
800-656-hope(4673)

About the Author

Born on May 3, 1982, in Frankfurt, Germany. To parents who met in Germany while Timothy's father was stationed with the U.S. Army. Timothy has dual citizenship, because his mother is German. At the age of eight, Timothy moved with his family to Stockton, California where his dad was raised. Timothy's life was one of turmoil and secrets. Living with a father who turned to alcohol and often sexually abused him, Tim quickly learned how to escape his abuse through temporal fillings of sex, alcohol, and pornography. He would later move to Hawaii, through his enlistment into the Navy where he met his current wife, Dawna and her daughter Sophia from her first marriage. His life was introduced to the Love of the Father, by his going to church with them. He then submitted to a healing process with Holy Spirit that would root out many areas which had traumatically affected him. They both began serving in ministries in the local church and God set them on a path of redemption! His mission is to partner globally with

Holy Spirit to show the Love of the Father to the fatherless.. Tim and Dawna have helped minister to men and women who have struggled with porn and sexual addiction along with identity issues through their ministry Visual Testaments. God has used their testimonies as a tool for helping others in their recovery.

Tim and Dawna have served in several ministries to include Evangel Cathedral in Spartanburg, SC and at Free Chapel serving under the leadership of Jentezen Franklin of Gainesville Ga. After eight years of local church ministry, they resigned to follow the call on their lives with Visual Testaments. They believe they are proof of the Power of the Holy Spirit in bringing Hope to the hopeless and the Father to the fatherless.

Get to know Timothy better at the following:
Visualtestaments.com
Facebook: Visualtestaments
Instagram: Visualtestaments

Made in the USA
Columbia, SC
17 October 2022